Stay Away From the Libertarians!

By Remso W. Martinez

Advance Praise for Stay Away From the Libertarians!

"Remso Martinez is a ball of fire! He has already earned a reputation as an indefatigable organizer and engaging podcaster. Now he can add insightful author to his growing roster of accomplishments!"

~Jennifer Grossman, CEO of The Atlas Society

"Remso is a politically savvy and well-thought-out American wise beyond his years. Peppered with humor in all the right places, Stay Away From the Libertarians! Is a fantastic look at our political landscape from an author with a colorfully honest and extremely articulate perspective. Get this book!"

~Dan Wos, author of *Good Gun Bad Guy*

"Remso in everything he does puts forth an amazing enthusiasm for the ideas of liberty and you get nothing less in Stay Away From the Libertarians! A fun and enjoyable story into what libertarianism is truly about."

~Alex Merced, former Libertarian candidate for US Senate

"Remso does a wonderful job of incorporating the principles of libertarianism with his own personal journey to the philosophy of freedom. This book combines humorous anecdotes with political theory, all while recognizing the realities of the world we live in."

~Tim Preuss, host of *the Tim Preuss Podcast*

"Most libertarians sit on the sidelines, congratulating themselves for how enlightened they are while they smirk and sigh at everyone else. If the libertarian movement grows, it'll be because of leaders like Remso and books like this, pulling the rest of us along."

~Dallas Jenkins, director of *the Resurrection of Gavin Stone*

DEDICATION

To Mom and Dad for always being so patient.

For the Lord who was there yesterday, today, and will be there tomorrow.

To persecuted people around the world whose names we'll never know, who crave freedom and self-determination.

~Remso W. Martinez

Table of Contents

FOREWORD

It was late one evening when my boss, Matt Kibbe, called me at home to ask me to speak to a group of students over Skype. He was sick and unable to make the appointment, but having recently witnessed me delivering a speech at a recent Students For Liberty conference, I guess he thought I was up to the job. Of course, I accepted, and that was the first time I met Remso Martinez, the enthusiastic leader of that student group asking me questions as I struggled to be understood through a dodgy digital connection.

A year later, I had the pleasure to be able to work with Remso directly, and since that time we have remained friends. I continue to be impressed, not only by his tireless efforts to advance liberty in America, but by his apparently unquenchable thirst for new ideas and points of view. I suspect the two are not unrelated.

Like most people who view human freedom as an end in itself, I have often wondered why this idea is such a difficult one to sell to the masses. All people, or most people at least, want to be free and resent restrictions on their ability to do what they choose. Is it not natural to extend the same courtesy to others? The Golden Rule, arguably the foundation of western morality, would seem to indicate so. Yet, there's the rub: not wanting to be a slave is pure instinct. Not wanting anyone to be a slave is philosophy. The question is, how do we get from instinct to philosophy?

If we look around, we can see clues that things are not as they appear, that something isn't quite right with the world. You don't have to be a sleuth to notice them, but you do have to pay attention. Why are there so many political slogans which people are required to repeat, whether or not they understand them? Why do people so ferociously root for one political party and demonize the other, when the policy outcomes are more or less indistinguishable? Why do we hate and shun people for nothing more than a difference of opinion?

Once you begin to ask these questions, you're halfway towards understanding American politics.

Let me put it a different way: why do people root for their hometown sports team? Why do people from Dallas support the Dallas Cowboys and people from Pittsburgh support the Pittsburgh Steelers? The players aren't from those cities. The coaches aren't either. Neither are the teams' owners. We've created the illusion that a group of professional athletes wearing the same colors somehow represents something special about a particular location, and people fall for it. Hard. It's the same reason the supposedly anti-war Left celebrated a Nobel Peace Prize conferred on Barack Obama, who proceeded to spend every day of his eight-year presidency at war. For the most part, these disputes are not about policy, they are about scoring points for your team.

In professional sports, thankfully, the stakes are low, at least as far as the fans are concerned. If the Yankees don't win the World Series this year, oh well, there's always next time. Fans may act like a Super Bowl loss is the end of the world, but they get over it soon enough.

In politics, despite the practical similarity of the two parties, the stakes are a bit higher. You may dislike Tom Brady, but no amount of Super Bowl rings will allow him to raise your taxes, throw you in jail, or regulate your livelihood out of existence. Government can do all these things with minimal effort.

Intellectually, people know that politics matters more than sports; it explains the sheer intensity of the anger and vilification of the other side, as well as apocalyptic claims that if our team loses, we might as well pack up the last 5,000 years of civilization and move to Canada. But I'm not sure most people really believe it. Like professional sports, I think it's just theater to most people, something to get outraged about, something to relieve the boredom of everyday life.

If people really thought Donald Trump was going to get us into a nuclear war, they would have been just as worried about Hillary, whose posture towards Russia should have been downright alarming to anyone who values life on this planet, instead of lionizing her as St. Hillary the Deserving. If people really thought Trump was a threat to women with his admittedly disgusting locker room talk, they would have, perhaps, shown the slightest bit of concern over Hillary's unapologetic defense of a known rapist (and I'm not just talking about her husband.)

It's theater. It's team sports. And the only thing most people really care about is what affects them directly. Once you've thoroughly internalized this, you'll realize that what we are engaged in is not, as is popularly asserted, a war between ideas. It's a war of an idea versus no idea. It's a prize fight between philosophy and instinct, and viewed in those terms, it's clear that no bookie in his right mind would give odds against instinct.

Yet, amazingly, the struggle is not a hopeless one. Mankind has triumphed over instinct before, the U.S. Constitution being perhaps the most impressive example. All it takes is for people to realize that they should want for others what they want for themselves, namely the liberty to decide how to live their own lives as long as they don't hurt people or take their stuff. The Golden Rule, as one would expect from so noble a substance, has not tarnished with age.

In the pages that follow, Remso W. Martinez (the W stands for "Winning") documents his own awakening to the philosophy of liberty, while simultaneously painting a picture of a dynamic and diverse movement, so different from the one caricatured in the popular media. We're not all born to be philosophers, but under the right circumstances, provided we allow our minds to be sufficiently open, we can all see that liberty isn't just personally satisfying, nor is it just the absence of oppression. It's a positive force for good for the entire human race.

Logan Albright
March 29, 2018
Washington D.C.

AUTHOR'S NOTES

Certain names have been changed for the sake of respecting the privacy of certain individuals. All remarks and opinions made are my own and do not represent that of any of my past or present employers or organizations with whom I publicly associate in any capacity.

Introduction

Politics for children and teenagers is all about who is going to win, and whether you choose to be on the winning team or not. Sadly, many adults have the same sports like mentality. After all, while each team at the Super Bowl has committed fans, you always have people sitting on the couch at home ready to become the biggest cheerleader for the winning team the next day. We aren't as sophisticated as a species as we like to think sometimes; we are all victims of our innate desires to belong.

I tried hard to be the smart kid when I moved to Virginia. My parents told me that the people where we were moving, due to our proximity to D.C. were wealthier and better educated than those in Texas and Kansas, where we had previously lived. This wasn't meant as an insult to the places we had previously lived. Instead it was said out of excitement for the opportunities that could potentially open up for my younger brother and I.

I was the new kid again for the third time in five years, and I knew very well that first impressions stick. I just wish my first impression wasn't "the new guy" because that nickname followed me through high school. Either way, I tried to make it apparent from day one that I was smart, so I signed up for the Technology Club where I could make model bridges, mousetrap cars, and build computers because I thought I'd look like Tony Stark and impress everyone. When making that decision in my pre-teen mind to choose a role model I didn't really think that decision through. I realized way later what made Robert Downey Jr.'s Tony Stark so popular was the fact he was cool and had swagger, major characteristics I did not possess. However I wouldn't realize that until puberty hit so I settled for being smart instead (NASCAR Club was an exception; I was the coolest guy in NASCAR Club because my predictions for races were almost always right). Immediately I signed up for honors civics, orchestra, theater, and the school news so I could further my advancement as a young renaissance man. This proactivity did get me lots of attention from my fellow students, just not in the way I had hoped.

In my mind, eighth grade was going to be the best year ever, but instead my plan to show my peers how smart I was ended in constant bullying, teasing, beatings, and even the theft of my gym clothes before gym class one day, leaving me with nothing but the pink loaner uniform that was a size too small, this led to the very obvious continuing cycle of bullying, teasing, and beatings to come. Still, as "smart" as I was, I missed the clues that maybe trying to be a teacher's pet all the time was the reason I'd get chased by bullies when I'd get excused from class to go to the restroom. This revelation didn't become obvious until I was hiding in a bathroom stall one day asking myself how I ended up in this crappy situation. Maybe it was because I talked my way onto the student council and attempted to become the homeroom dictator. But we'll get to that later...maybe. To an eager and young Remso, extra credit wasn't optional; it was mandatory because the dumb kids avoided it like the plague and the teachers always highlighted the students that put forth the effort.

By far the most enjoyable extra-credit assignment I remember was the 2008 Presidential election projects we were able to do in honors civics. To a young Remso, politics was awesome because one team in power could tell the other loser team what to do and if they didn't do it they'd get arrested. That absolute power always appealed to my middle school self because in my mind, maybe one day I could be President and send the guys that gave me nipple twisters and stole my gym clothes to Guantanamo Bay to get tortured.

The instructions were to put together a binder about either Barack Obama or John McCain regarding things like their biography, some articles, and why we liked their platforms. I remember going home and asking my Mom who I should do my project on and she said, "John McCain because we are Republicans." To which I asked, "Is John McCain the guy that is winning or losing? Because I want the guy that's winning" just for the sake of winning. All we had to do was bring some actual campaign memorabilia from our candidate of choice to class and we'd get full credit.

I asked my Dad to drive me to the local GOP office to grab some buttons and fliers the weekend before the election when the project was due. We walked into the GOP headquarters, which was at the local strip mall, and from the way it looked, you would have thought it was the Enron office after the company went bust. Pizza boxes were strewn across the office, there were rows of begrudging high school students knocking out volunteer hours and senior citizens attempting to save their Social Security checks making phone calls looking stressed and tired stretched across the small office space. There was someone pointing at a map on the wall yelling as if he were planning the rescue mission from *Black Hawk Down*. My Dad and I just stood at the entrance looking around at the circus before our eyes, I looked at him and asked if it this was a normal campaign office. He turned his head to look down at me and shrugged

The Republican office manager walked over to greet us and, after a quick exchange as to our reason for being there, he gave me a handful of McCain/Palin material and wished us a safe drive back. "You think John McCain is going to win, Dad?" I asked while pulling out my Gameboy in the front passenger seat while he drove.

"I honestly don't know but looking at that office I don't have a real positive feeling," he said. I was a little stunned to hear that (my awesome powers of observation at work once again), so I turned the Gameboy off.

"What do you mean?"

"I don't think John McCain is going to win because it seems everyone really likes Barack Obama." While my project forced me to pay attention to what was going on with the election to learn about the candidates, I was only twelve. None of the issues really made any sense to me beyond what political team I was supposed to be on according to my friends and family.

"What do you know about Barack Obama, Dad?" I asked genuinely.

"I know he's probably going to be our next President, so we should just watch and see how things go," Dad said without taking his eyes off the road, as if he had rehearsed that line numerous times in his head to let it sink in.

"What if he wins?" Immediately thoughts of being called a loser and wearing the pink loaner gym clothes shot back into my mind.

"Let's hope he's a good President and he does a good job. At the end of the day it doesn't really matter as long as he loves our country and wants to do what's best for it."

"Yeah, as long as he does a good job it doesn't matter if we wanted him to be President or not, because the President just wants to help the country," I said with a feeling of relief, mentally taking a step back and seeing this as more of a sport instead of a play for power. Election night was a week later, and Barack Obama just completely wiped the floor with John McCain like it was going out of style. "I hope Barack Obama does well," I told my parents as the news anchors on TV began to cheer.

"Hopefully," my Dad said with a blank, expressionless face as he looked directly at our television screen in the living room. I went back to my room and played with my Gameboy. That was it, all the excitement was over and it was time to get ready for school the next day.

Fast forward eight years later, the country wasn't only far worse than when Barack Obama came into office, but now people couldn't even tell what bathroom they were supposed to go into (thanks, Obama). I was in a hotel room with two of my friends after attending a campaign victory party for a congressional candidate we worked for, watching the small TV at 3:30 AM on November 9th, 2016. A *CNN* panel literally broke down in tears as Donald J. Trump was declared the next President of the United States. Jacob, one of my friends in the room who was a Trump guy from day one, couldn't have been more excited. He turned over to look at me as I sat up in my bed, slack jawed, watching the screen in utter disbelief, as did most people.

"Remso, what are you thinking man?" Jacob asked with a large smile on his face. I took my time thinking of what to say next, but I'm pretty sure I had passed out from the sheer exhaustion of having worked 72 hours straight.

Honestly, I had no thoughts other than the guy from *the Apprentice* was now President of the United States. "Life will get so much stranger" I thought to myself. The thing was things weren't going to get any weirder than they already were. Life had already been weird since the day I decided to get into the political scene. Let me clarify further, life was normal and perfectly black and white until I met those damn crazy, brilliant, funny, infuriating, insane, rational, kind, callous, friendly, viscous, simplistic, and overly complicated bunch of activists, academics, stoners, gun fanatics, bow tie loving hippies and other rag tag rugged individualists called libertarians.

I'm writing this because it is apparent, the politics of personal destruction have bled deeply into our families and homes, and the movement to promote limited government and free markets has never been more vital in American history. The opportunities to make drastic and far reaching changes to our community, state, and nation have never been more realistic than they are now. However we can't assume we are going to "get tired of winning" as the President once suggested. When you look at historical data from previous elections, you understand that in the ossified two-party system we have today, the pendulum swings pretty consistently between parties in control. The false image this conveys is that America swings between periods of progressivism and periods of conservatism. This couldn't be further from the truth. One of our most conservative Presidents of all time was Grover Cleveland, a Democrat. Republican Richard Nixon, serving almost a century after Cleveland, is one of the most progressive men to ever set foot in the White House. Parties may switch places in the seat of power, but ideological switches are far more complicated to spot if you are a politically apathetic individual. Needless to say, you simply can't rely on politicians to be honest about their intentions, and I really hope this isn't the first time you're learning this.

One of the most divisive men in the political arena before the age of Trump was a country doctor from Texas who ran for president in what many saw as a suicide campaign. Congressman Ron Paul, who ran as the Libertarian Party candidate for president in 1988 and for the Republican nomination in 2008 and 2012, re-energized a movement that has changed the face of modern politics as we know it. His willingness to call out neoconservatives and Fabian socialists in both political parties on the national stage made him plenty of enemies in the establishment class, but also inspired a generation of freedom lovers who are changing the landscape of culture and policy today. Paul's efforts to promote social tolerance, free markets, a government so small it could fit in the Constitution, and individual liberty sounded alien to many voters, but to some it was the clarion call that changed the course of their lives.

Many commentators and public figures credit Dr. Paul with creating the "Liberty Movement"; the multifaceted movement of public officials, journalists, activists, and academics who promote what some seem as "radical ideas" (I call it just plain old common sense, but maybe I am crazy after all). I do admit that without the great one Ron Paul, there would be no Liberty Movement post-Bush administration, but to call him the father of the Liberty Movement is a bit inaccurate. To claim this is to say that libertarian principles aren't simply a new concept, but that they didn't have a place in the American political sphere until rather recently, buying into the progressive argument that the majority of Americans are and have always been, pro-government supporters of an interventionist nation. In 1980, President Ronald Reagan's historic victory against the American skid mark known as Jimmy Carter officially branded the Republican Party as a conservative party, which may seem strange now. For most of the GOP's history, conservatism wasn't just ignored by Republicans, it was skewered by those who failed to understand it or just outright hated the concepts of a government that respected individual rights. This movement, however, neither began nor solidified itself with the Reagan presidency alone. It began to come back to life in 1964 with a cowboy Senator from my home state of Arizona, Senator Barry Goldwater (also known as "Mr. Conservative").

Goldwater is without argument the first major libertarian statesmen of the 20th century, without whom Ron Paul or Ronald Reagan would not be able to make their marks on history. Goldwater's book in 1960, the *Conscience of a Conservative* took the political world by storm by simply putting together a concise argument for the reasons America was great to begin with, because of our culture's foundational love of free enterprise and respect for the individual. Libertarian and conservative principles were what made America great, and thousands of brave individuals in the past and present continue to represent the best parts of our American experiment. It is only in the past century (give or take a few decades) when the spurs of collectivism came out and several generations of Americans were taught that liberty was a childhood fantasy, not their birthright.

I believe the man who sparked the fire that birthed the first movement for liberty is one whose name is often ignored and whose impact goes unnoticed; Nathan Hale, the first Patriot casualty of the American Revolution. At age 21, when most young adults today are drinking "jungle juice" out of bathtubs and learning the basic skills of "adulting" (you can't make this shit up), Hale was executed for espionage against the British Crown of King George III. A graduate of Yale and an avid scholar of religion and philosophy, Hale was a true academic, becoming a teacher before he joined George Washington's spy ring against the British Army in New York.

Hale died without friends, family, or loved ones present. His last words were, "I regret that I have but one life to lose for my country" before the noose took his life. The amazing thing about that was Hale specifically said "my country," because an independent country wasn't even at the top of the minds of the colony's assemblymen and legislators who signed the Declaration of Independence. Many at the time thought once the British left, we would be a confederation of numerous states, which we were under the Articles of Confederation after the Revolution. Hale said "country" because Hale dreamed of a nation based on the principles of individual liberty. Thomas Jefferson said it eloquently after he left the presidency; he envisioned America as a "empire of liberty."

Hale died before the Revolution ever truly began, without having a feeling of what the future would hold. Without knowing whether his dream of a nation born and raised by a people who craved independence would ever become a reality. Without Hale's sacrifice, General George Washington wouldn't have felt the pain of severe loss seeing a young man who was such an idealist robbed of life so early, forcing him to restructure the spy ring that helped the Continental Army eventually win America's freedom from the British.

The classical liberalism of Jefferson and Madison, nowadays called libertarianism, is a philosophy and ideology that, despite its rich history and influence on

Western politics and culture, is still incredibly misrepresented and misunderstood by the masses. This deep and romantic worldview regarding the principles of liberty is often hated by both modern conservatives and progressives because of a staunch difference of worldview or because of the lies and slanders of those that would like the word to be removed from the dictionary altogether. Together, we'll begin to understand why civilized society at large is practically begging you to stay away from the libertarians.

Chapter 1: Communist High School Musical
"It's easier to fool people than to convince them they have been fooled." ~Mark Twain

"Wow you look so skinny, you don't want to eat that, but I will," said José on Monday.

"You're gaining weight, you shouldn't finish that," said Kim on Tuesday.

"I didn't have lunch. It is only fair you give me some of yours so I can eat too," said Steve on Wednesday. "Only greedy people don't share. I saw your mom packed you a Coke, don't be greedy." Steve was the biggest asshole. He'd just walk over and take your food unless you sat within sight of a cafeteria monitor. José worked his way from one end of the large cafeteria to the other throughout the week; he didn't hit the same people twice, which was smart so it never seemed constant. Kim went around the cafeteria once a day (got to give it to José, he was a much better con artist than Kim) and eventually resorted to name calling if he didn't get anything. I'm pretty sure he would go to the lunch line before it closed and steal from the trays when the cafeteria staff weren't looking. Seriously, how else would you show up to the table with a dozen hot dogs? One day I asked him why he stole food and he looked at me after shoving two stolen hot dogs in his mouth and said he did it because he wanted to, as simple as that.

"Don't you know stealing is a crime?" I said to him, not because I was worried about his golden status in the community but mainly out of shock because of his shameful actions and lack of self respect. The Catholic guilt I once held in my life was repulsed by his lack of morality.

"I don't care," he'd quickly reply.

"What about what God says about stealing?" I'd say to throw back a quick retort. The other kids at my table looked at me as if I, at age 14, said I still believed Santa Claus. One thing I learned from growing up in the Midwest was when in doubt, throw the "eternal damnation" card and those around you will quickly repent. I was laughed at, lectured, and ridiculed by the table where the nerds, geeks, band camp junkies, Honors and AP students tended to sit while exchanging Nintendo magazines and dueling Yu-Gi Oh cards.

"I'm God, I can do what I want," Kim said while laughing at me. His philosophical stance, which had perplexed me would have caused deeper concern for the final destination of his eternal soul in my mind, if food from his mouth didn't fly on my face as he laughed . To this day because of lunch thief Kim, I'm still a little disgusted by hot dogs. We were kids then, but even I know that people my age back then would say stupid stuff for pure shock value and a cheap laugh. Still, you can see very well the development of a worldview in children, teens, and young adults based off their own words, as well as their actions and justifications for them.

The kids that stole and begged for food in the cafeteria weren't poor or "food insecure" as we are taught to say today. I also didn't live in a school district that remotely mimicked the inner city of Chicago or Detroit. The kids I went to school with were far from the East L.A. *Stand and Deliver* cast we would watch whenever a substitute teacher put in the movie when they didn't want to teach. These kids, I remember specifically were the children of bank managers, restaurant owners, federal employees, defense contractors, and lawyers, so they had the opportunity to bring food or pay for it themselves. They chose not to because they liked the game of it all. They liked to go around and convince you to give away your lunch, not because they wanted to pour out compliments towards your compassion or generosity, but because they wanted you to think they deserved it and you owed it to them.

In 2008, after Barack Obama became President, attitudes in public school teachers and administrators generally began to change. I began to see the residual shock in my affluent neighborhood, seeing over time how the "Obama Revolution" as pundits were calling it, began to shift the mindset of teachers and staff in public schools and universities around the nation. I started my freshman year in 2009 at Centerville High School, very much in the beginning of the era of "everyone just be chill" with everything, as one of my stoner friends once told me. Social justice became the new fad for students because in their minds they thought they were in the same league philosophically as Barack Obama and his merry band of celebrity friends who were bringing "hope and change." Social justice didn't contain the same connotation back then as it does now. Social justice was just something that it seemed our country, especially our affluent community, just had to evolve into as we were entering a new age of combined politics and popular culture, which in essence was now the new American church.

You couldn't disagree with anything Barack Obama said or else "you were going against the will of the majority of the country," as an English teacher once told me. "We are a progressive nation that is dropping old traditional values that don't fit in with today. What worked yesterday or a few decades ago doesn't work now. We are more open minded and willing to solve things to help everyone," she said. I don't remember what this had to do with literature and Shakespeare either, but she took time to spend a good chunk of class discussing Obama every class period for the rest of the semester until she got tired of it.

Everything was constant nagging and every day we were force fed the latest liberal talking points. My English teacher wanted to spend more time lecturing us on the racist history of white America regarding segregated schools instead of teaching us the actual course content. In World History, we learned about the evils of Western Civilization and spent a semester instead discussing the positive impact of Islam on humanity and how the Enlightenment humanists stopped the intolerant, backwards Christians from destroying the world. One project from that class had us discuss the illegitimacy of the nation of Israel and another project put us in groups to discuss how to stop income inequality (the consensus for each group's answer before presenting their plan to the class involved taxing the rich, more government jobs, and abolishing banks). In the Student Government class I signed up for (essentially an honors class for how to eat crayons) we all received A+'s for simply showing up because we were graded based on things such as "attitude" and "cooperation" which are purely subjective because you were asked to rate yourself and then were rated by the peers in your assigned table group for the quarter. Of course everyone gave everyone else A's because you didn't want to appear mean, risk your own grade, or get beaten up. I remember having to put up posters for upcoming school events and spend countless classes struggling to hang giant banners in the hallways while the other kids in my assigned group would go hang out in the cafeteria or disappear to go do something more enjoyable, either way some kids worked, others never did, but everyone got A's.

I never felt comfortable with the forced conformity in school, but I couldn't tell why. Rebellion looked different compared to what we had seen in the grunge 90's and the punk rock 80's. It seemed in my eyes that the conformists all had long, ugly pseudo bowl cuts (later a peer would enlighten me and say "it's skater hair"), jeans they purchased with pre done rips at the knee and half their boxers hanging out like convicts. The ones that wanted to stick out had their hair cut short and wore clothes that fit. In the eyes of the conformists, they themselves were the real edgy dudes who made sure to carry around a brush to get rid of dust on the expensive Converse and Nike shoes their parents bought for them. It is crazy how joining the counter culture can make you into a cult-like conformist and simply keeping to yourself and appearing presentable made you a societal black sheep.

I knew my family was conservative and that my peers and teachers weren't, but I didn't know how to argue effectively or why I defended the ideals I held in the first place. You weren't taught conservative principles at school and you certainly couldn't get them from TV. My parents didn't discuss politics in length with us since my brother and I were still young, and unless I watched *Fox News* to learn what the boring Republican position on things was, to be on the right of any issue meant you weren't just openly rebelling against everyone around you but you also never had anything to back up your arguments. During my daydream adventures in Algebra class I always imagined myself going up against the Sauron's army from *Lord of the Rings* without a wall to hold them off, a sword to fight them, and all of that without remembering to wear my pants to battle.

Teachers and other students thought I was dumb and just liked to fight. I began to believe that about myself too because I couldn't help but argue, even though I never really knew what I was trying to disprove in the first place. I knew conservatism was meant to ensure and protect freedom, conserve the concept of the "American dream" I thought everyone shared, but "freedom" in Obama's first term meant not wanting to give people health care, being part of the greedy rich class that destroyed jobs and the housing market, and just to put a cherry on top, hating minorities. To say you were anything other than progressive meant that, to them, you might as well have licked asbestos covered walls for fun. It got to the point where my Christian faith and conservative ideals were under constant attack and I really had no form of grounding strong enough to continue to care. If I wasn't strong enough in my Christian knowledge, it certainly didn't help that I didn't go to church since 2005 and wouldn't read the Bible seriously until 2013. I just gave up and began to take what I was being force fed as fact. My worldview wasn't true, I was constantly being ridiculed, and nowhere was there any kind of back up for me. Add all of that to a confused teenage dude and what you get is a angry kid who feels his place in the world isn't accepted.

What kinda broke my patience was when I realized something that most 13-14 year old kids would never pick up on. It wasn't something I would be able to define until I was much older, but the thought had been placed in my head. There were three to four students (white middle class students, if that matters) in my morning classes that never participated in the Pledge of Allegiance, and that drove me utterly insane because as a military brat with a parent who had just served during "the Surge" in Iraq, I felt like it was a personal slap in the face to sit down during the pledge, but let's break it down first so we understand the context.

People like the NFL players, illegal immigrants in California, and progressive champions in our universities sit out the pledge or national anthem for one of two reasons; they may sound like exaggerations but what you learn is that there are only two categories of people that sit out: people that hate the country and people that hate God. What I was able to gather during my time in one of America's most privileged public schools was that it is perfectly respected to hate your country and hate God (notice how I say God and not "religion", I'll touch on that later). Anything that went against American values such as free enterprise, family, and limited government was totally okay with the students, teachers, and certain members of the administration. You know what you could never talk bad about? The government and certain religions (if you're confused, just hang on because things are going to get weird).

"Happy Ramadan!" came out of the speaker for morning announcements during the season of Ramadan every year I was in high school. There was a large Muslim population in my school and it has grown larger in my hometown since I graduated in 2013. To discuss Islam without reverence and praise landed you in metaphorical shark infested waters. The staff and teachers made accommodations for Muslim students and always discussed the greatness of diversity and how we should treat students who wore head scarves with adoration, but dare say "Merry Christmas" or wear a cross and you would meet with instant discipline from staff.

"Remso," one of my teachers pulled me aside in the hallway, "you shouldn't say that." He spoke softly as if he were in fear anyone would hear our conversation out of some false pity or fear.

"I shouldn't say what?" I was genuinely confused. I have a habit of swearing unintentionally, but as I was replaying the last five minutes of our conversation in my head there was nothing to alert me to anything worrisome.

"You shouldn't say Merry Christmas. Someone might be upset you're pushing your religion on them," he told me. I was actually stunned because this was blatant hypocrisy. We had to celebrate Islam in class but to be a believer in Christ was somehow like saying you had sex with a dog (which we are seeing the modern Left begin to accept as an alternative sexual orientation but that's a different topic). It was ok to say our country was a fundamentally racist, violent, unfair, sexist, Islamophobic, transphobic, theocratic wasteland of bigotry but if you say anything remotely critical of the Obama administration at all you could be accused of spouting "right wing insurgent" rhetoric (sophomore year was full of colorful SAT words for me to learn thanks to teachers that didn't just want to disagree with me but insult me in the process) that was grounds for a stern lecture in front of all your peers or being banished outside for the rest of class to sit in the hallway in shame.

This is the type of stuff people think only happens on college campuses, but here is the unmentioned and ignored truth: once you start to hit public education, school becomes way more politically polarized, and these kids are indoctrinated in progressive groupthink way before they become drunk college students and barefoot, man-bun hipsters with fake glasses majoring in French-Lesbian critique of American literature or Beyoncé (you can take a class all about the fabulous pop singer Beyoncé, go Google it). It starts in the public schools. They are the incubator for this morally relative lifestyle that embraces collectivism, and the attitude students carry with them is what you see when they get to college. All these socialist professors do is reinforce what these students have been taught their entire lives already.

Remember Kim saying "I am God?" Once assuming he gets to college, all his progressive professors had to do is teach him how to make that argument a more convincing one. His worldview was taught at home and at public school, but his college professors fine tuned and sharpened it into a weapon of rhetoric. I think conservative and libertarian campus activism is in a sort of renaissance currently, but it only hits the surface of the real issue at hand, because while it may be possible to convert some Left wing students to the ideals of liberty, some are too far gone already and there is sadly nothing to be done short of a *Men in Black* style memory wiping.

Earlier I said that progressives didn't care if you openly hated or showed disdain for the United States, but would lose their cool if you spoke ill of the welfare state and the Obama administration. On Veterans day in 2012, the school had a tradition of holding a quick ten-minute ceremony before class started where they would read the names of parents still serving in the military, and would then have the student choir sing the national anthem. As one of the vice principals read aloud the day's speech from the office of the President, all staff and teachers present demanded absolute silence. When it was

19

time for the national anthem however, four to six students got together near the choir to mockingly screech and scream out the lyrics to mess up the choir who was obviously distracted, and none of the staff or teachers did anything to stop this disrespectful and ludicrous behavior. I asked a teacher standing nearby why no one said anything to the group of morons trying to screw up the anthem and I was given some bullshit talking points regarding "free speech" and "they were protesting the war in Iraq." The truth is no one knew why they were so disrespectful, but the point I got was that no one cared because it was okay to hate and disrespect the country. Yet, to ever show anything but reverence and adoration for the progressive messiah Barack Obama and his administration was outright sedition.

"The problem with communism is it just hasn't worked. Income inequality is bad, no one should have more than anyone else, we are all the same," was what I heard in my AP US Government class in 12th grade in 2013. These students believed wholeheartedly in the progressive cause because that is the only worldview they were taught to believe in. If you are an atheist, you can attack Christians and Jews for their faith, but don't go after Muslims because that would be racist (even though Islam is a religion, not a race). The rich are greedy and should share with the rest of us, and if they don't, their money should be taken from them by the government. The biggest problem in America today is that the government doesn't have enough power, the sort of power it has in Europe where our moral superiors are showing us what it is to be happy and prosperous. If you believe in traditional values, you're hateful and need to be more "open minded." By the way, the student that said communism hasn't been implemented properly? He was the president of the school's Young Democrats and went on to the University of Virginia where he got a commission in the US Army because he wanted to be "trained and ready for the revolution." He was also Korean, so guess how disgusted I was coming from a Korean family to be hearing rhetoric in the United States from a Korean that obviously ignored the existence of North Korea.

Life has changed so much in so little time when you step back and really look at things. In 2008, a popular substitute teacher came to our civics class and we did a quick lesson regarding the election. "Barack Obama isn't a socialist. No one wants to be a socialist. The Democrats just want people to be able to go to the doctor and not worry about the bill," she told me after someone reiterated what their dad had heard on talk radio. In 2015, I saw that substitute teacher on social media getting into an argument with someone I knew, and she shot back with, "We need socialism. Capitalism hasn't worked." Later, I went to her Facebook profile to see that she had attended a Bernie Sanders rally in Manassas, the town next door. So that explained a lot.

To make matters even more depressing, I had asked a long time female friend of mine on a date when she said, "I can't date anyone that isn't a progressive", so imagine how 16-year- old Remso felt when immediately the dating pool seemed very, very empty.

My high school mascot was the wildcat, so obviously the running joke was that Disney's *High School Musical* was based on us. I remember nearing graduation in 2013 when a few friends of mine were walking together in the hallway and we passed our graduating class mural which was being painted. "I heard the possible class quotes are down to two choices for the mural," my friend Chris said. I was curious, so I went ahead and asked, which in retrospect showed me that sometimes you just shouldn't ask questions whose answers might disappoint you. "What are they?" I asked.

"Whoever controls the youth controls the future," Chris said, "and I forget the other." I stopped walking. I felt like I had been punched in the gut.

"Dude, that's creepy, and I'm pretty sure it was a bad guy in a movie who said that, like Megatron or Voldemort."

"Well, yeah, I mean, it's Hitler. I did a Google search and he's every result." We both stopped and looked at each other. I honestly don't remember what ended up becoming the class quote for the mural, but now whenever I think of my high school I think of *High School Musical* and Hitler combined, and that's not a mix you want to think about when you're trying to have a pleasant day. It goes to show that when it comes to history or just the basic evidence of reality, all you need is to be young and impressionable enough in order to become completely indoctrinated.

For a good chunk of my generation, sadly, everything is just about perspective. Heck, it even makes that song *We're All in This Together* seem like it's pushing some type of ulterior motive at this point.

21

Chapter 2: Mitt Romney's Worst Volunteer
"Politics is a herd mentality" ~Gov. Gary Johnson

High school sucked for more reasons than just the forced politics. It also just happened to be high school, so use your imagination. I never joined the football team. I didn't do a school musical. I never attended prom or homecoming (even though I was always on the class planning committee, so you're welcome, everyone who attended and had fun). So, needless to say I felt like going into senior year I had to make up for some of the stereotypical pinnacle moments some people feel like they had to accomplish thanks to every coming of age high school flick ever made.

My small group of friends and I looked at the calendar and began counting down the days until we become real adults after our senior year. Our mentality from high schoolers to legal adults naturally turned our focus to the world around us. Questions like, "do you do taxes or does the government just handle that?" and, "which college has the most women so the odds are better and they have to lower their standards?" came up often. The first major adult privilege of our lives came during the mother of all elections, the 2012 Presidential campaign, or as the media remembers it, the time that rich Mormon who wanted to kill Big Bird tried to oust our first black president. 2012 was the last true great period for Democrats in recent history, because they could call everyone who didn't vote for Obama racist and horrible, and get away with it.

I remember going on a single date with a girl I had graduated from High School with one summer, and somehow the topic of that election came up. I mentioned how I had hoped for Romney to win, and I could have sworn she puked a little in her mouth. "Oh my God, I'm a Republican and even I voted for Obama because I'm not racist," she said. Being a gentleman, I still picked up the check and drove her home, but the inner me was screaming, "Wow, you are dumb and I'm totally not calling you back."

Anyway, I needed to be competitive for schools and scholarships so I knew that an easy way to make myself look good was to do some extracurricular stuff in the community. I needed a volunteer gig or something I was interested in, so I could see it through long enough to count. This was when I first ventured into the realm of politics, or more accurately my first failure-to-launch kind of moment.

I had spent the summer of 2012 mowing lawns for my neighbors, so I understood that to get money for comics, you had to go out and make it. It was hard; not only was the weather crap in Virginia but my neighbors had this dog that had demonic craps they never picked up and which I was constantly mowing over or stepping in. One time, I learned what a real "shit storm" was because I mowed over one of the dog's turds and crap went flying everywhere. It was like a slow motion scene right out of *the Matrix* and I never understood how far feces could fly. Another time, I stepped on some and I had to go wash off my shoe with the hose in my front yard. At one point I scratched my face after washing my shoes but something smelled terrible.

22

The horrid smell of dog crap was still around me, but I couldn't tell where it was coming from. My clothes were okay and I had just cleaned my shoes, but that's when I realized the smell was right under my nose. Literally, it was right under my nose from when I scratched my face and I screamed so loud I think I woke half the neighborhood with, "There is dog shit on my face! Please kill me, God, please." Needless to say, I valued my lawn money immensely and wasn't quick to listen to anyone that was saying I needed to pay a penny more for anything.

The potentially radioactive dog crap wasn't what began to morph me into an authentic conservative, however. It was the influence of someone the liberal media had deemed more dangerous than radioactive poop, Glenn Beck. The summers mowing lawns taught me to value my money, but what taught me to value things like free enterprise and constitutionalism were the afternoons I'd spend in front of the TV after school watching Glenn Beck on *Fox News*. Beck was like the Bill Nye of news and politics in my eyes. Far before he mellowed out and became the soft spoken grandpa over at his network *TheBlaze*, Glenn was far more theatrical, with his claims that the Michelle Obama sanctioned food changes for public schools would lead to "friots" (french fries plus riots, long story) and that Agenda 21, the UN program that would forcibly relocate people into eco-friendly plantations, was going to kick us all out of our homes. Beck pulled me back each and every day to sit in front of his magic chalk board, and I was hooked.

On August 28, 2010, Beck held one of the largest rallies in American history; the "Rally to Restore Honor." At that point it was probably the largest Tea Party rally in the movement's history and brought more people to the Mall than MLK had decades earlier. My Mom took the lead and took our family out to D.C. to watch as thousands of Americans of different backgrounds, races, and creeds stood together to proclaim that our government wasn't listening, and that only regular people had the ability to put things back in place. Anyone that knows my mother knows she is not one for loud noises or crowds, but my typically apolitical parents wanted to show my brother and I that there were so many others that had the same core beliefs as we did. After that fateful day, I was hooked on the news and the Beltway buzz like a bad crack addiction. It wasn't that I was inherently interested in the political process however, it seemed that conservatives only cared about things when election time came around when they could potentially change things, and allowed the progressives to control the day to day narrative the rest of the year.

What interested me was that Beck was able to paint a picture or tell a story to draw the viewer in. This is a skill very few people have, where you can take a far out scenario and make the listener feel like they have an emotional connection to the story, as if they were a character in it. I loved the fact that the Left hated Beck, because he was beating them at their own game and showing open defiance against their monopoly on narrative. He didn't just strike back at their loose claims and fiction peddled as reality, he always came back armed with the truth and an arsenal of facts behind him. In my view,

Republicans in office never got anything accomplished (it's fair to say even now they are incapable of getting anything done even when they have control of the federal government) but Beck was able to effect actual change through the sheer size and engagement of his audience.

In late 2009, Beck opened the floodgates on Obama's Green Jobs Czar Van Jones[1]. Van Jones was a devout believer in the Black Power movement in his youth and had declared his affection for communism quite publicly in the late nineties. In 1992, Jones was arrested for participating in the L.A. riots that came about after the Rodney King verdict. During his time in jail Jones became familiar with other black nationalists who taught him about anarchism and Leninism. In the mid nineties, Jones became an active leader in a anti-capitalist, racially charged organization named STORM[2] (Standing Together to Organize a Revolutionary Movement) whose role model for their utopian dream was none other than Chinese Communist Mao Tse Tung, who killed forty-five million people during the "Great Leap Forward". In 1999, Jones was arrested again for rioting during an anti-free trade event in Seattle. Somehow though, this Maoist who once wore Black Panther garb and military apparel for almost a decade had rebranded himself as a peaceful social justice warrior and climate change activist in the era of Obama, easily landing a job in the administration. No one even cared about Jones' open praise of Philadelphia cop killer Mumia Abu-Jamal[3]. Even though his time in the administration was short lived, it was long enough to get his foot in the door in media where he now has a cushy job at *CNN* like most former Obama officials and staffers. I can't rag on *CNN* as much as I'd like to, after all *Fox* did bring on Marie Harf who blamed the rise of ISIS on climate change and the lack of job opportunities. Marie, if you ever read this, Syria is in a freaking desert and a prolonged civil war tends to be bad for business, but it's not like your boss had anything to do with egging on that situation...

Because of Beck's fiery exposure of the facts, Jones became such a PR nightmare for the administration that he left his position within a month. This was by far the biggest blow the Obama administration suffered during both terms, because it was popularly driven with no way to fight back. It wasn't achieved at the ballot box or by a congressional investigation, it was accomplished because of the pressure of Beck's audience and sheer force of will only a mainstream media outlet could provide at the time. The Left will stick together no matter what and will always refuse to admit fault in anything, so for Jones to leave either by "suggestion" or on his own accord showed that the heat was too much for them to bear. Because of Beck's transgressions against the Left's great leader's hand picked minion, he had to be punished. For numerous reasons, mainly issues with the late *Fox* Chairman Roger Ailes wanting Beck to slow down, Beck

---

[1] https://www.youtube.com/watch?v=Q3czvyXsM_4

[2] https://www.realclearpolitics.com/articles/2009/09/13/how_could_obama_have_hired_van_jones_98293.html

[3] https://www.theblaze.com/news/2011/12/07/30-years-later-da-drops-death-penalty-against-cop-killing-black-panther-mumia-abu-jamal

ended up leaving *Fox* to go take a break and start *GBTV* which would eventually become *TheBlaze*. With Beck gone, there were few individuals anywhere who carried even an ounce of his energy and creativity.

At *Fox*, *Redeye* with Greg Gutfeld became my new crutch. I would record the show on my family's DVR, wake up an hour before school and watch an episode before I had to get going. *Redeye* was not an inherently libertarian show, though Gutfeld identified as a libertarian, but it did offer a range of rotating guests such as Andrew Breitbart and *Stossel* producer Kristin Tate (who I jokingly urged to run for president in 2017 on an episode of my show when she came on) who would always keep my attention with their talk of the culture war and free markets, with some cat videos in between. Gutfeld called out everyone and always pursued the absurdity of every story in the news, on the Left and Right. Most importantly, he was funny and no one could deny he was catching on with younger people. This need for a conservative Jon Stewart as producers tried to brand him, is what got Gutfeld on the hit show *the Five* and eventually his own day time Sunday slot, *the Greg Gutfeld Show*. Gutfeld in his shows and books has always mixed the absurd with rational thought to show how irrational we as a society had become. When Gutfeld left *Redeye* however, his tone changed and the punk rock attitude that *Redeye* itself was known for began to fade. Insiders told me it was one of *Fox News'* highest viewed shows at the time it was cancelled.

Television failed to show any conservative willing to stand up for anything. All we were provided were Karl Rove and Karl Rove wannabes, and interchangeable white paper pushers speaking on things no one cared to hear about. Based on our presence in popular culture, it was easy to buy into the the Left's claim that all conservatives were boring. You still see it today to a lesser degree if you look at young Republicans in any formal event where they dress like they are going to a 1960's prom and Jimmy Stewart is gonna show up and teach them how to be hip. The universe had a wonderful way of showing me where I needed to go however, and as I tuned out of the TV I discovered the internet.

Steven Crowder is still, in my humble opinion, the father of the modern right wing punk movement. This French-Canadian child voice actor turned stand up comedian who took a bold step of entering the realm of political satire and commentary as a conservative showed young people that you can be right wing politically but still cool and funny. Men like Crowder and James O'Keefe of Project Veritas fame showed that video was a necessary platform for a generation of young people that may have listened to conservative talk radio with their parents, but didn't engage with the content and certainly didn't walk away fully grasping their talking points, much less wanting to share them with their friends. This group of wild pranksters and funny philosophers sprouted numerous careers of other activists and journalists, and inspired others to carry their torch. Without men like Crowder you'd have no Milo, without men like Beck and Andrew Breitbart you'd have no Ben Shapiro, and the list (thankfully) goes on.

The one thing everyone I listed has in common, though, is that while they were all hated deeply by the progressive Left because they defied identity politics and media orthodoxy, they had universal appeal to politically apathetic young people who wanted to be entertained and informed. They represent disruptive platforms that break away from typical means, but above all call out hacks and scammers on both sides of the aisle. There is a reason Romney never once did an interview with Glenn Beck in 2012: it was because Romney hated him and what he represented, someone that didn't toe the establishment line.

Because my interest in politics was closer to the Tea Party protesters and internet punk commentators than the Republican Party apparatus and dudes going out of their way to dress like premature grandpas, I began to learn very fast that conservatives and Republicans don't necessarily overlap.

Because the GOP showed it would rather go hang with moderate Rob Portman and be seen at parties with RINO (Republican In Name Only) Jon Huntsman, obviously it didn't matter if I was seeing other people as well. What the progressive Left doesn't understand is that most conservatives will be the very first people to admit that the progressive Right is a thing too. These faux moderates cry out for their love of guns, babies, religion, and fiscal responsibility when they run for office but then get elected and become whores to special interest pimps and big government policies that go against every principle we think conservatives should hold dear.

When it was time for me to choose how I would be spending my afternoon extracurricular activities, I chose to pursue my new love of politics by signing up with the Mitt Romney campaign to be a volunteer for the local GOP. I call myself Mitt Romney's worst volunteer for the same reason I don't ever put that volunteer slot on my resume, because I did absolutely nothing. For the record, I did end up becoming a sports announcer for the school's athletic department, which was by far a better use of my time and even birthed my love of broadcasting which would eventually lead to my podcast. Back to topic, how could I be Mitt Romney's worst volunteer if I didn't do anything? And why didn't I do anything when everything was pointing to this having been a potentially great opportunity for a young and budding political nerd like myself?

Mitt Romney was not inspiring and he represented the boring brand of the GOP the likes of Crowder, Beck, and Gutfeld constantly reminded us not to emulate. The only reason I remember my Mom even getting excited about the election was when Paul Ryan was tapped as Romney's VP pick (Paul Ryan was a Republican folk hero at the time, much like Jeff Flake whose political career matches Two-Face's plot line in *the Dark Knight*). My mom even took us to a Romney rally in Manassas when Ryan's selection was announced because we thought with Ryan on his team, there would be less defending and more punching back in the campaign. Obviously we were sorely mistaken, because America's crazy uncle Joe Biden mopped the floor with Ryan at the VP debates, causing many to lose faith in the Romney-Ryan campaign entirely. Compare Mitt Romney to

Donald Trump and Paul Ryan to Mike Pence; Trump never defended anything and he pummeled everyone and everything into the ground, good or bad depending on your view on any situation. Romney, on the other hand, was far from a fighter, and backpedaled and apologized for things he didn't even say or do.

I signed up to volunteer and when I got emails asking what I would be interested in doing, I'd click on everything and show up for none of it. The little fighter I was in school was getting tired of the constant harassment for being the only non-Obama lover in class. I always emailed my supervisor with excuses as to why I couldn't make a single phone call or knock on a single door. As I looked at the correspondences with the supervisor and the other volunteers, I realized very fast that while these people believed in what they were doing, I wasn't willing to do more than wear a Romney shirt to school and argue with anyone who wanted to pick a fight. I was internally beaten, but I still needed to save face for whatever that was worth.

"Racist, sexist, Islamophobic, xenophobic, homophobic…" I was verbally harassed by teachers and students on a daily basis during that election. One thing I realized about the two students in my high school that were Romney volunteers was that they always conceded when confronted with something and never took a firm stance on anything. The one thing I felt I could do to contribute was to be dumb enough to never back down from an argument and say what I knew would set people off the most. I began to realize that I defended Romney less, and conservative principles more and more.

Because I was still on the email list and would respond in the group messages to say I wasn't able to attend something with the local GOP because I had to announce at a football game or something, I quickly gained a reputation, and not one to be very proud of. Yes, I was the most vocal conservative in my classes. I was everyone's token proud Republican acquaintance, but I was not accepted by the active Republican volunteers because not only was I not really doing anything active in the campaign, but I also was openly willing to criticize Republicans, a cardinal sin in party politics. I began to realize that I wasn't just Mitt Romney's volunteer in name only, but I also wasn't a very good Republican.

Just like a scorned partner in a poisonous relationship, I knew that if the Republican Party would openly cheat on conservatives with Beltway hags and faux moderates, there was nothing wrong with me seeing other people and willing to be seen with them too. While driving me to school one day, my mother had *WMAL* on the radio (the D.C. metro conservative talk station) and I was introduced to someone who became the Fonzie of my world before he became the bane of my existence four years later. Governor Gary Johnson of New Mexico, who I had seen in the 2011 GOP primaries make the joke that his dog had made more shovel ready jobs than the Obama administration, was back on the scene. I liked Johnson, and what I remembered of his short run for the Republican nomination was that he didn't care about peripheral issues that only mattered to certain groups of people. Johnson was a big picture guy who wanted to fix the economy, get us out of the war, and respect the privacy of people to live their lives as they wanted to as long as they didn't interfere with the peaceful existence of other people. To me, Johnson made sense and I didn't know anyone who had strong negative opinions of him, unlike Ron Paul whom everyone regarded as a joke candidate with "crazy" ideas.

I assumed Johnson was on the radio because he was out pushing for voters to show up for Romney, I was dead wrong. Johnson was on promoting his third party candidacy for the office of the President as a Libertarian. At the time, I was confused and thought he said "librarian" so I asked my mom what a librarian was doing running for president and she was as confused as I was. I saw Johnson on TV only once before the election after that radio appearance, on *the Daily Show with Jon Stewart*. Johnson labeled himself socially liberal and fiscally conservative (these days I gag a bit when saying those words out loud) and that he wanted a government that would respect the Constitution and the rights of people to live free. I didn't like social conservatism for the same reason I couldn't stand progressivism, because I didn't want people to tell me how to operate every single moment of my existence. If I wanted it I'd ask for it but instead some people just want to force it down our throats like foie gras every five minutes.

The older I got, the more I couldn't deal with these cultural puritans telling me how to behave. When Democrats jumped on New York City Mayor Bloomberg's anti-large soda crusade, I bought Big Gulps for a month. When anti-cigarette commercials began to get flat out weird, I started advocating the removal of anti-smoking zones on my college campus. If you told me not to do something simply because you didn't like it, it just made me want to do it even more. At one point during undergrad, my university banned swing dancing, so I drove around campus blasting *Footloose* from my stereo (something else you weren't allowed to do).

Johnson appealed to me because he was a big picture guy who brought up the elephant in the room. While the GOP nominees in 2011 were discussing who hated gay marriage the most and why drug users were a bigger threat than the Taliban, Johnson looked like the adult in the room. Silently rooting for him against Romney was my dirty little secret even though I was under no illusion that he had a shot of winning or making a dent. Gary wasn't the only force pulling me away from acceptable conservatism and Republican orthodoxy; it was also a dead Russian chick named Ayn Rand. In case I didn't mention it earlier, I had a habit of being interested in things I was told weren't socially acceptable (probably why I always argued for conservative stances even though I didn't always really believe in them). I once had a US History teacher who gave me two different lists of books towards the end of the year, books to read and books to avoid.

Let me rewind a bit. This teacher told us three things we needed to know in order to succeed in the class. According to him, US history should show the minorities and immigrants of the world one thing, "never trust whitey" (I'm part Asian and Latino and even I knew that was racist. It's like saying "don't trust the negroes" or "don't trust

Chang"). Secondly, "no flag waving patriotism, America has and still has problems and isn't worth celebrating." Lastly, "Republicans don't like blacks, women, education or the environment, but above all they love Ronald Reagan who was a moron so what does that say about them?" I was constantly put on the spot and forced to answer for every conservative crime in the world. He once asked who my parents wanted to be president. My dad was in Afghanistan in 2011, and I knew my mom liked Newt Gingrich and Rick Santorum so I gave him those names. "Gingrich is just like Bush: he took credit for everything Bill Clinton did and let's not forget he also cheated on his wife. And Santorum? Not only does he not think black people aren't equal to white people, but he hates gays and women." All slanderous accusations and none of them true, as I would figure out.

      I just sat there and took it, I had lost the will to deal with the teacher's constant bullying. I started the year sitting in the front and slowly began moving farther to the back of the class whenever we had the chance to change seats every quarter. At one point I said I liked Jon Huntsman for the same reason the Left loved him, because he wasn't a conservative. Lying to give him that concession I knew would get him off my back to some degree. I knew one positive trait was that he was a voracious reader so I asked him what books he recommended I read during the summer. He happily obliged and recommended four to five books (thanks to him I read *Doctor Zhivago*, which is one of my all time favorite stories. Still not a fan of *Seabiscuit* though). He did, however, say there were some books I would be told to read by "the wrong people" so he recommended books to avoid that might come up in "my circles" (I had like all of two conservative friends so I don't know what circle I was in outside the comic geeks). What was funny was that he copied his list to give to other students too, and that I would end up being the only person of the bunch to read them. He had remarked the previous week that if I actually enjoyed reading, I would have read the textbook and my grades would be better. I always felt like looking at him and saying, "Sorry, maybe if you didn't constantly single me out to be the butt of your jokes I'd be more interested, but I have to deal with you, try not to constantly think of my deployed father, and also come to school and not get beat up or my backpack tossed in the trash while asshole Steve is eating my lunch."

      I walked into class one day and he pointed to me and said "Remso, you know what today is?" to which I replied, "Tuesday."

      "We just pulled the last of the troops out of Iraq. You can thank Obama for ending the war. Now do you like him?" he said with a smirk. I wasn't a foreign policy expert but I was at least able to point out at fifteen years old that the Arab Spring in 2010 wasn't a "Democratic Revolution" or "Muslim reformation" as my teachers were calling it (for which I was called racist, Islamophobic, and stupid) and that things were probably going to get much worse (spoiler alert: they did).

      "He can say it's over, but it's not really over" I tried to say under my breath so he couldn't hear me speak.

"Remso, stop being a denier. Osama is dead and the war is finished." He finished talking, smiled confidently, and began to teach class. Looking back at that moment I wish I could go back in time with a newspaper that says "ISIS" on the front cover. Sometimes it takes time to have the world prove to you that you're right and all you need to do is sit back and be patient.

On the list of books he gave me, he told me to avoid Ayn Rand, "what is Ayn Rand?" I asked while scratching my head.

"Ayn Rand is a person and you just shouldn't read her books unless you want people to think you're a dumb dumb," he said. That was it, that was all he had to do to get me to do the opposite. I was in the library and at the local bookstore gathering up as many of Rand's books as I could. I bought them because it pained the progressives. I read them because they told me not to, and simply possessing the books in my mind made me the biggest badass in town. What was ironic was that he probably brought up Rand because at the time copies of her magnum opus *Atlas Shrugged* were flying off the bookshelves at rapid rates during the Obama years. "Going Galt" and "Who is John Galt?" were on the back of stop signs and on bumper stickers around town and I didn't put two and two together until then. Even bigger, Part One of the film adaptation of *Atlas Shrugged* had come out in select theaters the year before and Part Two was coming out pretty soon, and only hard core libertarians and Tea Partiers were particularly excited because for once there seemed to be a "anti-Obama, pro-conservative film" as one blog called it.

It seemed weird, though, because as I was getting into Rand, popular Republicans and conservatives seemed to be running away from her as she was just about to be embraced by the entirety of the right wing. Paul Ryan, Romney's vice presidential pick, was being attacked by the Left viciously for saying *Atlas Shrugged* was one of his favorite books. Ryan, like most spineless Republicans, pulled a St. Peter and denied Rand in public to atone for the sin of embracing someone politically incorrect. I was so confused, because even now other Republicans on TV and online were trying to avoid Rand at all costs and telling others to do so as well in order to avoid looking "extreme."

Now even people who are supposed to be on my side hated this person and her work too, which made her all the more taboo, making me more enticed to check her out. I watched the films, read *the Fountainhead* and *Atlas Shrugged*, and then things became clear as to why this dead Russian immigrant was still so divisive.

"She believes that capitalism should be celebrated and that man should seek out his individual pursuit of happiness by living the life he desires because he wants it, not because others tell him to want it," I told a friend of mine while trying to explain the thug notes version of Rand's philosophy.

"So, she's against socialism?" he asked.

"Yes, she was against communism, socialism, and big government in bed with crony capitalists who work with government to rig the market," I replied.

30

"So, why do conservatives hate her?" now he was getting confused.

"She basically didn't buy into the religious right stuff, where they try and get their personal beliefs into every political or social decision. She viewed that as coercion."

"Oh, so no wonder the religious right isn't a fan of her."

I wish it were that simple, and for me to get into everything in order to do her justice would require for me write a completely different book entirely, so I'll try my best to condense it as much as possible. I read Ayn Rand for the reason so many apolitical, lonesome and angsty teens read her books, because she was taboo and being taboo was part of my identity. Rand's characters all had similar traits, all were loners who were raised and brought up in a system where they were told to conform, and that the purpose of their life was to serve others. The self-anointed elite taught that the worth of the individual was solely based on their worth to "society", and that no person was more important than any other. You learn the biggest lie in the world in preschool, and that lie is that we are all the same. Yes, we are all the same in the sense that all life is equal and precious in the eyes of your Creator. That is the Judeo-Christian belief. But even in Christianity we are told that though we are equal in the eyes of the Lord, we are all different, unique, and set upon our own paths. Progressives will tell you all people are equal and worth the same value to society, and maybe to a impressionable teenager and a Tide Pod eater that makes sense but when you break down progressive "equality" it is anything but "equal."

Martin Luther King jr. once said that people should be treated based on the content of their character, not the color of their skin. If Dr. King were alive today, the progressives would most likely call King a dumbass, a racist, and most likely an "Uncle Tom" as they have called Republican Senator Tim Scott, brain surgeon and former presidential candidate Dr. Ben Carson, and famed singer Joy Villa (the hatred and praise she received for wearing a MAGA flag as a dress took the internet by storm), and so many other remarkable people. In the secular progressive worldview, there is a hierarchy, and it gets very complicated very fast.

First, what should be decided is whether you were deemed worthy of life to begin with. In "liberal land," as we'll call it, if you're not wanted, your mother apparently has the right to kill you based on convenience. This is why I've never bought the "rape exception" for abortion argument, because what it says is that people conceived through rape aren't worthy of life and aren't equal in societal standing to children who were conceived in a healthy, intentional manner. Essentially, the exception claims that there are two types of humans:, the ones that deserve life and the ones that don't. This is similar to the Dred Scott Supreme Court case, which decided essentially that black people were property, not individuals with free agency. If you're lucky enough to not be split in half, dissolved with acid, or sucked through a vacuum in the womb, you are worthy of life, which then gets more complicated.

The politically correct caste system is tricky. If you are a white male you have been born into a automatic life of privilege because of ancestral sins against indigenous people and therefore must atone for your existence by hating yourself (go online and search "soy boy." It's hilarious). If you are a white woman, you are above white men but lesser than minority males and females, because you are still white. Because of degrees of "oppression," Asians are above whites, latinos are above Asians, blacks are above latinos, and Muslims are above all people as long as they are of Middle Eastern or North African descent. Gays trump straights, but are still beneath Muslims. Transexuals are above homosexuals. Muslims are still on top regardless, and I don't know where pedophilia goes because the progressive are still writing the book on that. I have friends of all sexualities, ethnicities, and backgrounds, and this social justice hierarchy is offensive on a human level, as it implies some people matter more than others. Coming from a Christian perspective, all people are worthy of the same respect and rights that come with being human.

Back to Rand. She was a secular humanist, but believed we have inherent natural rights because of our mere existence and ability to come to logical conclusions about the world around us. Value should be based on one's ethics and ability to produce and prosper in a free market absent unjust force and coercion. Instead of celebrating victimhood, Rand believed what should be celebrated is progress and production. In her mind, should we celebrate the man making steel for the railroad and employing thousands of people and making the world better, safer, and more efficient? Or the poor person who is complaining that he or she should be paid $15 an hour at McDonalds? Rand would say the producer, not the beggar, looter, or complainer.

Most importantly, Rand's characters lived a life of intention and value, something that doesn't mix well with the secular progressive "truth is subjective, everything is relative, life is meaningless" crowd. Howard Roark from *the Fountainhead* was disgusted by the character of Peter Keating, because Peter didn't know what he wanted to do with his life. No one understood Roark because all he wanted in life was to build his own buildings for the sake of doing so. In *Atlas Shrugged*, Dagny Taggart wanted to be the best CEO, because she wanted to be able to make a profit and display excellence in difficult times, while Hank Rearden wanted to make money for its own sake, while being his own boss. Equality 7-2521 in *Anthem* wanted to create, invent, and obtain knowledge because he refused to be subjected to the life of a lowly street sweeper.

Rand's philosophy focused on the power and value of the individual and warned of collectivist tendencies, and for that she has committed the ultimate progressive sin, rejecting the notion that some people are more special than others because of superficial and hollow reasons. On top of all of that, before Rand I had never encountered such a fierce defender of laissez-faire capitalism and property rights. For once, I had encountered someone who told me I didn't have to justify my existence to others. A school guidance counselor once asked where I wanted to go to college, and I gave some excuse like the Air Force Academy or Harvard, something like that. "Maybe you should lower your standards in life and consider community college for a few years to find yourself, Remso," she said with a straight face. I don't remember why I was in her office, but I was pretty floored that a grown women would tell a decent kid to lower his expectations in life.

From Rand's defense of capitalism and rational selfishness, I was introduced to a whole new school of thought that said money was not the root of all evil, but in fact the best human creation in existence because it was the peaceful and mutual exchange of value for value. Above that, no one had to apologize for doing what they wanted to do for their own ends. I remember shedding a tear when I first finished *the Fountainhead*, because for once I found something that was a near perfect representation of my beliefs and values as an individual.

There was a catch, though. Objectivist thought is a set of principles, but Objectivism, as Rand would teach, was also a systematic worldview that has some aspects you have to accept completely in order to buy into the rest. I was a cultural Christian as a teen, but I wasn't willing to rule out an existence beyond ourselves, as Rand wanted us to. The religious right will say Rand hated religion, but what she hated was the existence of any religion that tried to teach that the individual had no value. Rand herself had written speeches for Barry Goldwater with plenty of religious fervor because she understood our identity as a historically Christian nation. I knew early on that while I believed in most Objectivist principles, I could not label myself an authentic Objectivist since I rejected the tenets of the Objectivist worldview regarding the base of objective reality Rand described as the crux of everything. With that said, I was finally able to at least zone in on my core beliefs beyond basic cable news styled conservatism. I was becoming a libertarian, the one thing everyone around me warned me to avoid.

"You can't be a Republican and not be a conservative, Remso." A guy at lunch told me.

"What if I'm a conservative and just not a Republican?" I asked. He just looked at me as if I had stuck my tongue to a frozen flagpole.

"Dude, you sound confused," he said. Nope, I knew what I believed. Now the task was simply finding and understanding the words that had Rand finally begun to throw my way.

Chapter 3: How to Lose to Liberals
"Ridicule is man's most potent weapon" ~Saul Alinsky

In war you are killed or imprisoned, in polite society you are censored or ostracized. Romney lost badly against Barack Obama, so the narrative the media and the Democratic Party painted was that the American people had spoken and that they love Obamacare, massive stimulus spending, appeasement to hostile regimes abroad, and had wholeheartedly rejected the conservative ideals the right had supposedly campaigned on.

I saw Romney's defeat as a golden opportunity however to come in and take the place of those who admitted open defeat. There was a former Catholic priest and current philosophy teacher at my high school, who was rumored to be a shameless conservative. I had to meet this man, this metaphorical Bigfoot in the wilderness of the progressive forest. I had to find this person who could potentially be the Gandalf to my Frodo and find a way to show other students you could be conservative and proud. There was a Latina heritage club, an ebony heritage club, a LGBTQ club, and the Young Democrats, so I was going to make not a Young Republicans club, but a conservative student group that specifically cared about conservative principles first and foremost. I wanted to show other students who were afraid to come out against statist dogma that just because you lose doesn't mean you are wrong.

I emailed this instructor and set up a time to talk to him in his classroom about two weeks after the election. We sat down and I told him my plan. Without a second's hesitation, he said, "Well, I'll make it easier for you, I've actually put in the paperwork with student activities to form one just in case a student ever showed interest." I was stunned, I felt like this was meant to happen and that by Divine Providence this was what I was meant to do. Announcements went out, I put up fliers, and our first meeting was about to happen a week later. I was so excited for this to finally happen I didn't sleep the night before. I was the first one to show up to the room, and within ten minutes before the orientation meeting started the room was full of over forty young self-identified conservatives. I felt like this was going to be something amazing, but looking back, I'm glad the whole thing burned to the ground and had the earth above it salted.

The first matter of business was the club's own undoing. We had to hold elections for president, vice president, and secretary before we could actually decide on an agenda and calendar for the rest of the year. Because I was not the person who submitted the formal paperwork to start the club, I was not the automatic president since it was started by a teacher and not a student. The members took a vote and chose to hold the elections a week later. I declared I was running for president and over the next week I worked my heart out. I was going against three other people, a freshman who dropped out three days later, a cheerleader who openly said, "My parents told me I'm a conservative so I guess I am", and a guy who turned out to be a real asshole (I'll get to him later. He actually did me a favor, I honestly forgot his name so let's just call him "the Asshole"). I

34

went to other clubs to caucus their support, I made posters, and my running mate for vice president didn't just happen to be a second generation American of Indian descent, but he was also the only Muslim conservative in our class. It was the winning ticket. We were a diverse team that brought the energy of a Tea Party attitude to the table, and things were looking great.

It was election day, and I was going up against the Cheerleader and the Asshole. This time, sixty people showed up to the meeting to vote. We gave our speeches, and not to float my own boat but I think I did pretty well, because I got an actual energetic round of applause for the first time in my life. Things were looking great, and after the Cheerleader flopped, I thought I had it in the bag since the Asshole was essentially unknown. He walked up to the podium holding one of my fliers and laughed, "This is why they hate us..."

I was screwed.

"Remso doesn't understand that the people have spoken and we need to stop pretending that government doesn't have a place in our economy and our lives. I'm the secretary for the Young Democrats and my sister worked for Elizabeth Warren, and I'm here to tell you I've seen the other side. If we just meet them in the middle we can actually win, but we need to accept some truths: we have to tax the rich and talk about sensible regulations on guns as well. The people have spoken, the Tea Party lost, and we have to be mainstream if you ever want to win again." He finished talking and the room was quiet. "No more rabble rousers using fiery language to fire up people who don't represent the majority of the country," he said while pointing at me. I was sick of it, and without thinking I stood up and cut him off.

"Attacking me is not a campaign!" I yelled, feeling like a man taking a stand, but in reality I was a kid throwing a temper tantrum, waving my fist in the air acting like a man who was losing and in denial (retrospect is a bitch). Pretty quickly I was shouted down, and inside I felt a man melting into a boy, I let my frustration get the best of me. He smiled, walked back to his seat, and my running mate looked at me and said "Remso, we are screwed." The votes were cast. I received twenty-seven votes, the cheerleader received three, and the asshole got thirty. I was devastated, I lost to a full on and open progressive who was now the president of the Young Conservatives.

"We need to win. Obviously something is wrong with conservatism and maybe we should listen to what the liberals are saying," one person told me.

"The majority of the country told us we were wrong, so maybe we should learn to be right," another one said. I felt like I had been pimp slapped in public. The Asshole walked around smiling and shaking hands. The teacher came over to me and said he'd hope I'd stick around and not let the loss prevent me from coming to meetings. I lied and said, "Of course I'll stick around," and then I never went back to a meeting again. I thought about going to a debate between the Young Democrats and the Young Conservatives, but it made me feel awkward so I went home instead. According to some dudes who went, the conservatives conceded every argument and at one point the Asshole admitted, "Capitalism doesn't work." I was told about a year after I graduated from high school the club died out. I was glad. It was an abomination of Frankenstein proportions.

Think about it; how much damage did not just the Asshole inflict on the conservative narrative, but also the people that voted for him and stuck by him? I'm not upset at the Asshole primarily because he was, well, an asshole, but the thirty people that said "I'm with the Asshole" totally bought what the Asshole was selling. What was conservatism? They couldn't answer it, and even if they gave an accurate answer the Asshole probably shit all over it.

"Wow, Remso, we haven't seen you in a while," a friend of mine said one afternoon. I had been going directly home and staying home after school a couple of weeks after that election.

"Yeah, people have been making fun of me saying I sucked so badly I lost the Young Conservatives election to the secretary of the Young Democrats," I replied. In my defense, I actually had gone to a Young Democrats meeting when I was campaigning to propose the debate idea (which the Asshole stole). Long story short, all I got out of it was that cutting *PBS* funding meant I hate poor people, I wanted to bomb everyone, and opposing abortion on demand meant I hated women, so needless to say it wasn't my crowd. Oh, remember the kid I mentioned in the first chapter who said communism just hadn't been implemented correctly? He was the president of the Young Democrats, and later in life I was told he became a big Bernie Sanders bro. The narrative everywhere was clear, conservatism was a placeholder word for "empty."

I was upset, disappointed, but mostly confused. This didn't feel like a regular high school election where the popular guy wins. It was strange because for the first time in my life people I didn't really know who were members of the club were begging me to come back. I could have gone back to be the leader of those that saw things my way, I could have probably ran for president again, I could have made a name for myself another way, but I didn't, I just didn't want to go back and pretend I was okay with things. Call it pettiness, call it pride, it doesn't matter because that's what I did. I went about the year trying to pretend I was okay.

In 2015, I started my first semester at Liberty University where I got my BS in US Government Politics and Policy. In one of my classes regarding the study of the Executive Branch, my professor stood in front of the class and asked us, "There is an obesity crisis in America and it's your job to solve it, and you're all congressmen, so what do you do about it?" You'd think you'd get some federalist scholars and free market believers, but that wasn't the case at all.

"We should ban being fat!" I kid you not, someone seriously recommended that. One student then recommended creating a committee to adjust Obamacare, requiring that obese people pay higher rates (think about it, conservatives who liked and wanted to weaponize Obamacare). Yeah, Liberty University has been called the most conservative

36

campus in America, but that class was a microcosm of authoritarians and aspiring little dictators.

"The government has no role in trying to get people in shape," I said. The professor gave me a thumbs up, so at least he was on my side. I mention all of this because something became abundantly clear to me over the years, anyone can call themselves a Republican, but there is an open secret that it doesn't matter whether you are a conservative because not even conservatives are willing to define or defend their values. The editor of a popular conservative website and I spoke at length about this issue once, with him claiming the Republican Party alone was less about promoting conservatism and more about being anti-progressive. I was lost after that high school election in my teenage angst and moodiness, putting myself in a pitiful mindset. This was the best thing to ever happen to me though because everything that came later came out of that moment.

I went to the bookstore with my parents and bought a copy of *Reagan: The Notes* which was a collection of quotes from Reagan's notebooks and journals. I needed to know how to justify and defend my beliefs so I knew studying Reagan would get me there. Somewhere down the line I was researching his 1976 campaign and I came across an interview where he stated, "the heart and soul of conservatism is libertarianism." I was stunned, there was that word again that I'd seen pop up way too often.

I can't go back and change history. For the next year the Young Conservatives created a narrative that the Tea Party was full of religious zealots, Romney was too conservative, and all solutions for life's problems could be found in the federal government. If I couldn't own the narrative in that moment, I was going to make sure the narrative of tomorrow was dictated by me and those like me. I look back now and realize how insignificant that whole episode was, but the interesting thing was that high schoolers were essentially debating the issues of the relevance of conservatism when the actual adults were doing the same. You look back to 2012 and the deep and thorough venom of politics seeping into even teenage culture showed things would only get worse down the road if the kids, who should have been worried about graduation, cars, and dating, took the time to actually argue politics.

I used to look at highlights of the 2012 debates where the other candidates and moderators would dog pile on Ron Paul, the only person in the room saying something that wasn't being parroted by everyone else. Sitting in front of the TV, I felt like joining in the crowd in a sense. "Why the Hell is he on the stage saying crazy stuff like that?" I would ask my Mom. Now I finally understood not just why Dr. Paul was getting booed, but how if felt like to be one man against the crowd.

How innocent things look in retrospect, and social media wasn't even a big deal yet...

Chapter 4: Put the Kitten Down!

"It's now authoritarians vs. libertarians, since Democrats vs. Republicans has been obliterated…" ~Matt Drudge

After the defeat of Mitt Romney and a whole slew of Republican up and comers in 2012, the Republican apparatus was already looking for the folks that it believed would be the young guns of the GOP. Chris Christie (aka "Get Your Own Beach"), Paul Ryan, Marco Rubio, Jeff Flake, and Eric Cantor were some of the top picks people always listed off. Somewhere online, though, there was someone named Justin Amash who popped up on my screen. In the article, the writer mentioned that this freshman congressman was going to become the heir to the Ron Paul wing of the House of Representatives. Up until that point, I thought Ron Paul was the loony old guy from Texas who wanted to abolish everything and legalize drugs, prostitutes, drug addicted prostitutes, it seemed whatever he saw in life he wanted to abolish or legalize.

The only time I had ever watched Ron Paul intentionally for more than maybe two minutes was when he appeared in the Sacha Baron Cohen film *Bruno*. In that scene, which you can find pretty easily online, Cohen, who portrayed the gay, European model/ journalist named "Bruno," tricked Dr. Paul into a interview where he proceeded to try and "seduce" him, and instead managed to freak him out and cause him to flee the room. It is probably the funniest two minutes of your day you can manage to carve out if you want to watch one of the most ungodly and obscene things related to Ron Paul.

Learning more about Amash, he just didn't give off that radical vibe that I thought of when I thought of Ron Paul. Terms like "libertarian leaning" and "independent minded" were used to describe him, and "party outsider" was used pretty often as well. I began to sympathize with Dr. Paul and Congressman Amash, not for ideological reasons, but because the words people used to describe me such as "radical" were thrown at them on a pretty regular basis. What I did see pretty fast was that Amash seemed to represent the same things I believed in, the things that made me feel like I was the only one in the world who thought them. Things such as, if you're going to go bomb some country, you should probably get Congress to declare war and not spend money you don't have. Rumor had it at the time that at one point in Amash's life, he too had become disenfranchised with the Republican establishment and had gone home in a fit of disappointment and simply typed his ideas into Google. Amash picked the first things that came up to see whether or not he was alone in these thoughts or if there were others. Somehow, this strange Republican ended up coming to the realization that he wasn't just a extremely conservative dude, but was in fact a libertarian. There was that word again! Why did it keep coming up? I didn't have anything against libertarians, but at the time the only one I knew of was Gary Johnson and his example of fiscal conservatism, social liberalism. Some people kept referring to Ron Paul as a libertarian, but he was a

Republican, and as far as I knew, only conservatives could be Republicans, wasn't that the point of parties?

I thought if Justin Amash could just Google his ideas, I could do the same. It was like an overdose of information, I'm pretty sure I didn't leave the room for a weekend except to eat and crap. Hayek, Mises, Rothbard, and Friedman were shooting up on my screen. I watched hours of YouTube videos describing what libertarianism was. That weekend I had taken some lawn mowing money I had and bought a "Ron Paul Revolution" t-shirt to formalize my conversion. The language which had once seemed far fetched coming out the mouth of Dr. Paul now seemed to be like a second language for me. I felt like Neo from *the Matrix* after getting unplugged and went to school the following Monday feeling like the most morally righteous person in existence (yes, now I was more annoying than before). This time I didn't just rub the progressives the wrong way, now I openly ticked off the minority of conservatives and Republicans as well.

The day of Senator Rand Paul's "can the DOJ drone strike a Starbucks?" filibuster in 2013, you better believe I felt like a badass at school arguing with everyone in my AP US Government class. Above all everything just made sense for the first time. I realized that government wasn't the solution for every single societal problem, but the cause of most those problems. I realized that people should be free to live their lives peacefully as long as they don't use the force of the state as a mechanism to push their beliefs on others. The ideas of liberty didn't offer the answers to all of life's problems, but what they offered was the opportunity for you to chart out the course of your life without the fear of unjust persecution or restraint. I felt like Howard Roark in *the Fountainhead*, living life based off my chosen principles and opening my mind to the experience of life which valued the individual over collective group think and unchallenged authority.

Around this time I began to watch less Steven Crowder and more of Julie Borowski, the YouTube sensation that made libertarians a relevant force on the internet (and proved not all libertarians are old, white men). I started watching less Hannity and instead dedicated my viewing time to episodes of *Stossel* on *Fox Business* in a way which can only be described as religious conviction. As if I didn't have as much of a social life as is, you better bet I read *Atlas Shrugged* cover to cover that year. Needless to say, I felt as if I was the coolest person to be around with my urge to talk politics all day to a nauseating length. As I look back at teenage me, even I find myself incredibly annoying and am surprised even people who liked me and stuck around didn't beat me with a stick to get me to shut up about Ron Paul.

The thing about being a libertarian was that I felt this was the first time in my life I didn't have to juxtapose myself to fit one particular political worldview. I had gay friends in high school and I didn't see them as the threat to society some had. I had even began to question the war on drugs. At the time it wasn't not because I was buying the whole self-autonomy thing yet, but because it didn't make sense to send someone to jail for some pot only to have them come back and become hardcore gang members like something out of *Breaking Bad*. Above that I began to realize that if we wanted to make sure bad people didn't abuse their power, maybe the best course of action was to limit that power which had exceeded the boundaries of the Constitution.

Austrian school economist F.A. Hayek said it best: "If we wish to preserve a free society, it is essential that we recognize that the desirability of a particular object is not sufficient justification for the use of coercion." For too long, even I had bought into the belief that government force was needed to ensure your ideals could be applied to society. That's lazy thinking for anyone that still believes that, because if your ideas require force than they probably aren't good ideas. I won't tell you what to do in your church, so you sure as Hell shouldn't tell me what to do in mine, but at the same time I'll defend your right to believe whatever the Hell you want as long as it isn't impeding on the individual liberty of another individual. Freedom means you have to respect the ability for others to pursue their own definition of happiness, expecting them to respect yours in the process as well. Tim Moen, chairman of the Libertarian Party of Canada once said, "I want gay married couples to be able to defend their marijuana plants with guns," and I think that sums it up pretty well.

What all this began to show me though was that the "fiscally conservative, socially liberal" pitch was good for enticing new people, but you begin to see that phrase fall apart when you really begin to understand the principles of libertarianism. If we take that description at face value in today's modern political context, you can reach the basic conclusion that libertarians want government to cut the fat on spending and also just live a morally relative life, thus falling into fleeting, draconian concepts.

Being a teenager was hard enough, and now having this existential crisis of worldview was essentially pouring gasoline on a fire. You're raised and taught and force fed one concept of government, you either swing to the left or you swing to the right. On the right, you value free markets and guns and God but if you swing too far somehow down the line you become Hitler. I never understood, and still don't, how more freedom led to Hitler, but that's how it goes I guess. On the left you have efforts for more equality of outcome, socialized medicine, gay rights, but you swing too far and now you've ended up in Mao's China. It seems the only place to stay safe was in the nice healthy middle, where you never know where anything is going to go.

Was I a moderate? I asked myself that many times. I had friends who were gay who I never looked at and thought, "So this is what Satan created?" I had friends who loved guns and I never assumed they were in any which way or form inherently violent people. The thing about political moderates is this, they almost always lean left. Additionally, people who like to consider themselves split ticket voters aren't even really independents. If you grew up voting mostly Republican, you'll continue to vote mostly Republican, and vice versa. That isn't the controversial part, the controversial part is where I begin to talk about why I don't buy into the false neutrality or holiness of political moderates like John Kasich or even, dare I say, Bill Clinton.

I was sitting in a foreign policy class my last semester of Undergrad and a friend of mine and I were having a discussion regarding a moderate student we both shared a class with who we all labeled "Liberty University's token liberal" in jest. My friend looked at me and said, "You've got a conservative and a progressive arguing about a cat, the progressive wants to stick the cat in a blender, and the conservative doesn't want to stick a cat in the blender at all. A moderate comes by and recommends only sticking half the cat in the blender, and when the conservative screams about how little sense that makes, the moderate calls him a extremist and tells the progressive the blend the cat since he didn't yell at him." Why isn't a libertarian thrown into this cat blending conundrum you may ask? Well it's funny, I always assumed the libertarian was the cat, because the progressive obviously hates cats and the conservative is too busy speaking on the cat's behalf instead of letting the cat speak for itself. By the time the moderate comes in, the liberty kitty has accepted its fate that it's doomed to be ruled and led to an unwanted death by idiots.

Back to Hitler, why is it each end of this Left-Right roadmap to Hell always leads to doomsday? We may never have a solid answer why the Left-Right political spectrum is political science doctrine, but many have argued that it was intended to program young minds into picking one terrible side or another, or refusing to commit to any values at all in order for the State to remain the ultimate source of power. Either way, Left or Right, the cat is still at some point getting put in the blender. Some people such as David Nolan[4] saw this as an inherently flawed method to determine political leanings. Nolan, a founding member of the Libertarian Party, created an alternative to the Left-Right spectrum, which instead is 2D graph of a diamond that shows you the essential liberal-left and conservative-right in terms of values on the x-axis, but also the statist or libertarian tendencies of control or freedom running along the y-axis. It's funny if you look at it because people's heads explode when they see how close figures like "conservative" George W. Bush and "liberal" Hillary Clinton really are to each other.

All that time reading Ayn Rand and exploring the classical liberal school of thought from John Locke to Thomas Jefferson taught me that you shouldn't just mindlessly ignore the actions of others, but you have to understand that the need to protect life and property is the foundation of freedom. The rest of your worldview is entirely up to you at that point. You begin to see what the government refers to as "tax payer dollars" as your dollars and your family's dollars, that the actions and laws that limit the actions of some groups of people truly limit that of all people. If Reagan was right, than that meant that the purpose of conservatism was to be a force for the protection of liberty, and somewhere along the line we had forgotten and surrendered that holy purpose.

In terms of partisan politics, things became blatantly obvious where people began to draw their lines. The boundaries between progressive Democrats and moderate

---

[4] https://www.nolanchart.com/faq/faq8-php

Republicans became non-existent, and it appeared to be Rand Paul, Ted Cruz, Justin Amash, Thomas Massie and Walter Jones against the whole world of the establishment political class. New media godfather Matt Drudge tweeted out on September 3rd, 2013, that, "It's now authoritarians vs. libertarians, since Democrats vs. Republicans has been obliterated…"

Chapter 5: One Day We'll All Eat Zoo Animals
"Que sera, sera [what will be, will be]" ~old Spanish saying

Some things are processed by people in different ways, whether it's through the forms of reading, witnessing, or doing. For me, I'd rather read a book on Austrian economic theory than watch a dry and boring lecture about it from a man who looks old enough to have an autographed edition of the Bible. When it comes to certain things like understanding the history of fractional reserve banking and financial reform in the United States, I might not be very enticed to spend much time learning that at all no matter how it is presented, unless you have a beautiful brunette with a Afirkaans accent from South Africa present it to me in a all-expense paid five star resort in California. Then I might sit down and give my complete attention.

That example of the nice hotel I just provided actually happened, and I can't go further without mentioning that during most of the day they had a never ending bacon bowl available for every meal. I'm talking a never ending supply of crispy, mouth watering bacon that I still dream about years later. Frankly, I enjoy parties, weddings, and social gatherings a lot less if there is not a massive supply of bacon available on demand, but maybe I'm just spoiled because of my upgraded standards for comfortable living. Besides, I hear the more bacon you consume the less likely you are to be killed by a terrorist since the spirit of the pig the bacon once came from exudes from your body like a nuclear power plant in the presence of any jihadist, causing them to burst into flames when stepping within a ten foot radius of you. My freshman year of college in 2014, I applied for a chance to receive a Bastiat scholarship to attend the Cato Institute's annual Cato University, located at the beautiful Rancho Bernardo Inn in San Diego, California. This was basically a week of seminars that taught me everything about the law, history, economics, and philosophy from a libertarian lens I was never going to learn in school. The thing about the Cato Institute was that these guys and gals were (and I'd still argue are) the folks who put libertarian solutions on the table for actual lawmakers to see. During my time exploring the wild and wacky world of libertarian subculture, I had noticed that everyone from Rand Paul to Gary Johnson had credited the Cato Institute for one thing or another at some point in helping them draft or provide advice for important policy decisions. I was still a newbie in this movement, but the opportunity to get to listen to Dr. Randy Barnett from Georgetown Law, Dr. Tom G. Palmer from the Atlas Network, and so many other direct policy influencers, experts, and academics was like getting to go hang out with the Beatles.

Like all subculture movements, libertarians have their own role models and celebrities (often called "celebritarians" if you want to dig around a bit) and these encompass everyone from Ron Paul, Murray Rothbard, to a Libertarian Party National Committee member named Star Child. Dr. Palmer was like the Indiana Jones of libertarianism because he travelled everywhere, met everyone, did everything, and managed to speak more languages than you could imagine. Randy Barnett was the rag tag lawyer who had been fighting for drug reform for decades, and managed to be one of the few folks at Georgetown Law not to be a Marxist hippie. Think of Mark Ruffalo's adaptation of Bruce Banner with a Law degree, and that is Dr. Barnett.

I had been listening to the *Cato Daily Podcast* for about a year when I got to go to San Diego. To me the idea of a think tank was a place where people with four to five master's degrees go to write massive white papers for policy makers who would in turn, never read them and instead just throw them away. Essentially, it's a pretty accurate statement, but what you begin to realize when you learn the mission of a think tank like Cato is that an organization such as Cato doesn't just do massive policy reports so they can fight for a senator's attention for the sake of just a pat on the back. If libertarians have one big problem, it's that they suck at communication, and Cato mastered that where others failed. Cato gets what Cato wants, and it's that attitude that sets them apart from everyone else. In the realm of influence, the Libertarian Party screams, "I'm gonna be as eccentric as possible and if you don't like me, fuck you." But organizations like Cato say, "Hey there, you seem like an interesting person, let's go grab a drink!" Seriously ask yourself who you want to hang with.

When I go out and tell people I'm a libertarian, they usually ask me if I'm part of the same cult as the fat guy that stripped on TV for the world to see at the 2016 Libertarian National Convention, in what made the most interesting two minutes of television in *C-SPAN*'s history. If the world of internet chatrooms and social media are accurate (just humor me for a moment) then libertarians are mindless anarchists who have neckbeards and obsess over Bitcoin, pot, Jewish conspiracies, and anime porn while living in their mom's basement surrounded by a pile of Popeye's chicken boxes and 9/11 truther films. To be honest, I was kind of expecting that from not just the Cato staff, but the participants who would show up to this event. I'm happy to say that of all the people there who attended, only two had neckbeards, the rest were rather fashionable and attractive people.

At the check in desk for Cato University, I was greeted by two beautiful women who signed me in and gave me my room assignment. My roommate for the week was an Ivy League lacrosse player, and the two women who were in the room next to ours (I was convinced they were supermodels) were two political science students from George Washington University. One of the girls was a blonde from Texas and the other was a dark haired Latina from Venezuela. The speakers at all the lectures were very well dressed men and women of class who controlled the room with their charm and mastery of their fields. I wrote a blog for a fledgling website several years later where I urged Libertarian Party candidates to shower, dress appropriately, and stand up straight. The screaming and hate I received online for that blog was so mind numbing you'd think I said dogs should be able to vote or get called for jury duty or something else insane. The assumption that showering and owning one nice suit made you a sellout conformist was one I never expected. Regardless of generation, well dressed individuals command more influence and respect in any setting. I didn't say that because it was just a random thought that popped into my head one day, I said it because there had been candidates and activists I've met in my life who look like they sleep outside on a park bench, and then they wonder why no one takes them seriously. This week taught me an important lesson, appearances do in fact matter, because you don't just represent yourself but you represent everything you attempt to stand for. Thanks to the 2016 Libertarian Party National Convention streaker (aka "he who will not be named") an entire movement based on natural rights and individual autonomy was now tied to nudism.

During one of the lectures regarding banking reform, there was a girl who was attending school in South Carolina who sat next to me. She was probably the first libertarian woman I had ever spoken to so obviously I was stunned, beyond the fact she came over just to talk to me (it may have also been because the only available seat left was next to mine but I guess we'll never know).

"What do you think of the lecture?" she asked me. She was beautiful and put off an image of wealth from her dress down to her shoes and the manner in which she carried herself. I learned she came from a wealthy and politically connected family in Virginia. Last time I checked, I'm pretty sure she now owns a vineyard or something. She was different however from some of the other scholars because she wasn't here to network for a political run, push for a career in commentary, or the typical reasons you'd find. I can honestly say I attended because after a hellish year at a Marion Military Institute in Alabama, I wanted a vacation to anywhere (the attractive women sunbathing in the California sun, lectures on freedom, and the unlimited bacon bowl were just a bonus really). She kept talking about the "lifestyle of freedom" and honestly it just kind of flew past me. I was here just wandering and wondering where do I go from here while other young adults were finding donors for their future Senate runs. To have this young lady here just to enjoy the talks and the company for the sake of it seemed interesting, but it just didn't sit with me that there wasn't another motive.

"You can't be in this room with all these bright and connected people and not want something out of it," was what kept swirling through my head. The knowledge and networking I received from Cato definitely solidified my libertarian beliefs, but to deny that the opportunities that could come out of it weren't intoxicating would be a lie.

Remember how I joked about her owning a vineyard? This brilliant girl who could have written her own check to whatever career she wanted graduated the following semester and went to South America to work on a vineyard. She could have done anything, but she chose that whereas other people would have pulled out all the stops for power, popularity, and other benefits. She didn't match the hippie image of a free spirit I had in mind, but she had the mindset of intention, and she wanted to live life on her terms without having others bend over in order to accommodate her. She was the living incarnation of Howard Roark from *the Fountainhead*, and I didn't realize that years to come. Everything in my mind came down to the pitch, the "what do you really want?"

"Yeah, I'm totally into banking," I said. She looked at me and smiled. She could probably tell I was full of it.

"Well, this is the lecture for you then." We both turned to the speaker from South Africa and listened to the history of banking. Not going to lie, I remember nothing from that lecture other than that banks aren't your friends and you shouldn't let politicians get involved with your money. I was looking at my watch the whole time, wondering when I could run out to the bacon bowl. As soon as the lecture ended, the men in the audience ran over to "ask questions" to the South African presenter and I was on my way outside to the dinner buffet. I jolted over to the bacon bowl and before I could grab the tongs, another hand swiftly grabbed them. I don't know who this person was, but for that one act alone they had made an enemy for life.

It was in fact one of the other Bastiat scholars, a short brunette with cunning eyes, staring at the bacon bowl and holding the tongs as if she was mentally marking her territory. She had a lapel pin on the event lanyard that caught my attention. "Students For Liberty" it said, arching around a torch in front of a scroll. She passed me the tongs after grabbing a pile of bacon for her plate, I remember seeing her at the hotel gym while I was working out, she was doing Flash level speed on the treadmill at an inhuman pace, she could have all the bacon she wanted, I stopped being frustrated soon enough to ask about the pin.

"We're an international group of student organizers who help arrange events, start new clubs, and recruit others to engage in their campus and community," she told me, and then took a strip of bacon from my plate as soon as I noticed hers was empty (yeah, totally not cool. She was lucky she wasn't a dude). My excitement grew beyond belief. Never in a million years did I ever assume there was an entire student organization committed to advancing libertarian beliefs. Everything I had found online prior were dead Facebook pages that people randomly made for fun, ads for the Libertarian Party, or one of the millions of shrine like websites for Ron Paul. The "Liberty" movement that people kept referring to as it seemed didn't have a conduit for activism in a sense when I started learning more about all this crazy stuff. The adults in the room had political parties and their Tea Party organizations, but what about the rest of us? Were we destined to just scream into a void? SFL solved that problem.

I had a running partner back at MMI who was a politically savvy guy. We'd go off to the back road that led into the middle of the nearby farmland where the road stretched for miles uninterrupted. I didn't have much of a social life my first year outside of the corps of cadets, but at night I'd pull out my laptop and plug back into the world and explore all the events and moments I wanted to be a part of. This liberty-minded following I was pursuing outside the dictatorial confines of the Institute and the progressive utopia forming outside of D.C. near my home in Virginia,

"Libertarians will never win, man, there's just no point in getting involved with that stuff," he said after we finished four miles of sprints.

"What if we organized better? There are people in a void looking for those that care and they are met with either low standards, no resources, and few to no people to help," I replied. He smirked, as if he had heard all my complaints before.

"Gary Johnson got 1% of the vote in 2012. Ron Paul was universally ignored in the primaries in 2008 and 2012. Rand is cool, but it's a moment that is going to come and go. I'm not getting my hopes up," he said, and my feelings dipped, I felt he was probably even right until I got the acceptance letter from Cato and then ventured to California a few months later.

"Ron Paul was kind of quirky though," I said to kind of lighten up the mood.

"All libertarians are, Remso, I mean, we've been talking about this stuff for an hour last I checked."

You're probably thinking at this point I don't like Ron Paul, and the answer is I actually really do, it's just at the time unlike many libertarians, he didn't pull me into these ideas. I know countless individuals in libertarian and conservative circles who were brought in by one of the Ron Paul campaigns, but something about the way he spoke just didn't connect with me like it did with others. The thing I found during this libertarian moment everyone was talking about was the fact that now they were searching for the next Ron Paul.

Going back to California, a few friends I had made went down to the bar area the other students were hanging out in. The Students For Liberty chick I met earlier introduced me to several dudes from Venezuela. One was a lawyer and the other was a some kind of financial analyst who was starting a firm that would mine for something called "Bitcoin." They were having the time of their lives, and a whole group of us were just fascinated with the stories of what was going on in Venezuela as the country was reaching a state of hyperinflation. I couldn't believe the stories they were talking about. At one point they were complimenting our roads, literally, our roads because they were so well developed compared to theirs in Venezuela.

"Americans, you just don't see how good you have it at all," one of the Venezuelans said before slamming some cocktail with Red Bull. "You have it all yet you want to go ahead and strip yourselves of your treasure and dignity. It is almost as if history doesn't matter and you all think you live in a void. You don't care what goes on outside your borders. We can scream to warn you not to do what we do and you'll do it anyway." Things got quiet and a little awkward.

"I'm only a college freshman…" one of the other American students said, but the Venezuelan swiftly turned his sights on him before he could finish his sentence.

"I knew a guy who was seventeen and was locked up for criticizing the government. Your country was founded by men your age. You're not incapable of action, you're just scared of repercussion and you want someone to stand in front of you to take the pain so you can lob retorts from the safety of somewhere they can't hit." Everyone either went back to drinking or began to scatter.

Sometimes it seems even the most "woke" amongst us need to be brought down a bit. In 2016, I was interning at the *Newsbusters* division of the Media Research Center (MRC). My first day in, one of the reps from *MRC Latino* came in to introduce himself to me, just me.

"No!" I stood up from my chair as he reached out to shake my hand, "I know what you're about to say, I don't want to be a token Latino in the office, I don't speak Spanish and the vocabulary I do have is limited to the Taco Bell dollar menu. I'm happy to work in this section and want my work to be the only thing that defines me." The editors in my section just kinda stared at me with blank faces. I had totally misread this situation.

"So, that is great and I want to congratulate you on being an empowered minority..." This is when my face went pale and I realized I had really misinterpreted how this conversation would go. It seemed that in most circles I was accustomed to being the "token", especially in regards to matters of politics. "I just need you to monitor any reports from *CNN* regarding what is going on in Venezuela." I felt dumber now than I did twenty seconds ago.

"Uh what's happening in Venezuela?" I asked. Within the past eight months before I went to work at MRC for that Summer, the Socialist regime of Nicolas Maduro, the successor to the deceased Hugo Chavez, went overboard with printing money, creating a state of hyperinflation[5], and ended up finally destroying the Venezuelan economy. Rationing for food became so severe, a mob broke into a zoo in the capital city and began to eat the zoo animals[6]. Literally, if people in a civilized country have to resort to eating lions and tigers and bears (even a poor flamingo was a victim) why weren't we hearing about this on the news? Because the news didn't care and the only socialism we were allowed to hear about came from the mouth of the enlightened Bernie Sanders, who dodged questions about the crisis in Venezuela more smoothly than Neo from the film *the Matrix* dodging bullets like an absolute boss.

I walked out of the bar after the one Venezuelan gentleman managed to make everyone feel less than great. Walking back to my room, there was a terrace level with a great view of the golf course and surrounding area. Sitting there was a beautiful woman in a floral dress, reading a book alone in one of the wicker chairs. I had recognized her from earlier. She was part of the group of students from Venezuela. Right before going to California, I had just ended a relationship with a girl back in Alabama, so feeling the sting from that and now feeling less than awesome after having my first world privilege thrown at me by a drunk Venezuelan the size of a linebacker, the thought of enjoying a nice

[5] https://www.forbes.com/sites/stevehanke/2018/04/25/the-ins-and-outs-of-venezuelas-hyperinflation-spotlights-on-the-imf-and-the-financial-press/#793367c0103c

[6] http://www.breitbart.com/national-security/2017/09/05/venezuelans-eating-dogs-zoo-animals/

conversation with beautiful woman in one of the most beautiful locations in the country seemed like a decent idea so I could end the day on a high note at least.

"Everyone in your country is so nice," she said, taking a flower out of her hair, behind her left ear and placing it between the pages of her book to mark where she had left off. "I hope to come back here soon."

"What do you want to do?" I asked.

"Anything that will bring me back. Listening to all the speakers the last couple days has solidified that."

"But what do you want to do here?" I asked again.

"I'm open to anything, as long as that I am happy and can pursue whatever this country has to offer." There that answer was again, pursuit of happiness, words I thought only existed on paper written a long, long time ago.

Our time at the Rancho Bernardo was coming to an end. On the last night together, Dr. Palmer, Dr. Barnett, and a few other speakers brought all the students together for somewhat of a pow-wow in order to give us a proper send off.

"What was this week about?" Dr. Palmer asked us. No one answered so he just started pointing at people.

"Learning about classical liberal theories and history?" one student answered.

"No, you all are already smart or else we wouldn't have paid for you all to come out here," Palmer sat down in front of us in a chair facing the room and just stared for a moment into the crowd. "You're here to meet others, see the world from a different lens, and feel an obligation to be part of it, because everything is going to come around and affect you at some point, whether a state away or a continent away. Ideas are borderless."

I didn't get a chance to get to know every person who attended, but from just keeping an eye out I could see everyone who attended went on to make an impact to those around them, whether it was through policy, activism, academia, or even those that went on to simply live the freest lives they possibly could in order to maximize their own individual happiness did us all justice.

One gentleman who attended out of his own pocket was a doctor from Iowa running for US Senate under the Libertarian Party. He was a quiet, soft spoken man who didn't go around telling people who he was or asking for favors. Doug Butzier sat next to my roommate and I one morning at breakfast. A gentleman sitting across from Doug learned of his campaign and began to criticize his odds of success.

"You have a better chance of running as a Republican," the gentleman stated.

"Here is the problem, sir, I'm not a Republican. I'm a Libertarian," Doug replied. My roommate and I laughed at his sly comeback.

"People aren't going to consider voting Libertarian anytime soon, so we have to move the needle some way," the gentleman said. Doug took a pause before responding.

"Maybe I can move the needle my way," said Doug. He knew he wasn't going to convince this man to change his party or to change his opinion, so the most he could do was kill him with humor. Doug had a silent Calvin Coolidge-esque manner to him, and we got along rather well. Several months later, I asked Doug to Skype in as a guest speaker to a student group I formed, of everyone I had asked to speak, he was the only one that said yes.

A month later, Doug was going on a hunting trip with a friend and flew in a small private aircraft. A week before the speaking event my group was hosting, Doug's plane crashed on the tarmac and he died on impact. Managing this new student group was difficult enough, having Doug die suddenly made everything seem so much worse. In a stroke of fate, I managed to get a new speaker local to the area, and on the night of the event, the room had around sixty eager students who came to listen.

I walked up to the podium and before I addressed the crowd and our guest, I took a moment out for Doug. That day happened to be election day 2014, and Doug's name was still on the ballot. Some people run campaigns as the protest vote candidate, people vote because they just want to give a finger to the world. Doug, in death, received more than eight-thousand votes that day. "Don't ever let anyone tell you the odds," I channeled my inner Han Solo, "life, liberty, and the pursuit of happiness isn't just a cute phrase for politicians, it is in fact the inherent goals for people who crave freedom and their ability to live their lives without asking permission to be themselves. Some people take action even when they know the odds are against them, and they offer themselves to loss, sacrifice, and ridicule because they know someone has to."

Libertarians often don't like Thomas Jefferson's addition of "pursuit of happiness" in the Declaration of Independence, because they feel it undermines Jefferson's inspiration from John Locke who coined "life, liberty, and property." Honestly I'm not interested in picking a preference, but what I will say is that the "pursuit of happiness" isn't defended enough in mainstream discussion. Happiness is inherently an individual emotion that only each person can describe uniquely to themselves. We often spend so much time fighting for tangible causes that we ignore what it is to be human, to know of our own impending demise one day but to nonetheless live, love, and laugh.

You can't measure happiness as a collective, there is no magic formula to ensure maximum happiness for everyone, you have to create and protect an environment where people are free to discover their own happiness as long as they do not infringe on the rights of others. It is elementary, it is basic, and it is fact, not one man or collective can define individual happiness. Therefore, we have to fight for the chance for others to discover it themselves. I take it back, I think I like Jefferson's choice of words better.

"I don't know where you all want to go, but go with a sense of purpose. Freedom is a lifestyle," Dr. Palmer said, looking around the room. He dismissed us and we all were about to walk out when the South African speaker from earlier that day came around the corner, dressed in a stunning cocktail dress and red heels.

"Who's going to go grab a drink with me?" she said. Every dude ran outside. We think "freedom" and the big things come to mind- voting, speech, religion, the press, etc.

but sometimes, here in the comfortable United States we take our opportunity to have fun for granted.

What's funny is that four years after I attended Cato University and two years after I was done with my summer at MRC, I was doing an episode of my show with my friend Morgan Zegers, an inspiring young woman running for New York State Assembly at the time. She mentioned how in college she had a roommate who was a communist, like a serious, Marx loving, Lenin reciting, Soviet propaganda posters in her room communist. Morgan and her lived peacefully amongst each other and they would debate respectfully from time to time.

"What about Venezuela?" was Morgan's trump card when debating her roommate's communist utopia.

"You all love to bring that up, don't you?" the roommate would reply.

Chapter 6: The Youth in Revolt

"Educate and inform the whole mass of people… they are the only reliance on the preservation of our liberty." ~Thomas Jefferson

"Community organizer" usually brings to mind for most Americans "drug dealer" thanks to the strange introduction to Chicago politics America was shown during the 2008 election. "Student activist" doesn't bring many positive things to mind either. If you ask my parents, or any conservative parent for that matter, "student activist" brings to mind the Kent State massacre where the National Guard shot at student protesters rallying against the war in Vietnam. The less extreme answer sometimes given is the stereotype of a angry hippie activist with a megaphone yelling at people going about their business on campus because they feel they can change the world if they scream at enough people.

In a conversation with Kassy Dillon from *Lone Conservative* on an episode of the *Remso Republic* podcast, we went back and forth throughout our talk discussing whether or not students are generally firm in their political beliefs by the time they reach their freshman year or not. Kassy stood by the assertion that many are either apathetic or willing to listen, while I took the stance that people would rather claim they are right about something they don't believe rather than be seen as weak because they are willing to change their mind. Looking back on that conversation however, I realize one thing is without an argument true, that those impressionable college years can without a doubt convince a person to take steps they otherwise wouldn't take if they were outside of a group of like minded peers in something akin to the college environment, away from home for the first time encountering things you otherwise wouldn't have been exposed to.

A dangerous example of this is a dark history is so terrifying that the Democratic Party and the progressive movement wish could be swept under the rug. Even before WWI, socialism was creeping into American politics rather openly thanks to the industrial era's new labor and progressive movements brought on by the likes of William Jennings Bryan, Samuel Gompers, former Vice President Henry Wallace, and others. The Intercollegiate Socialist Society, founded in 1905, eventually turned into the League for Industrial Democracy (LID), who created a youth component called the Student League for Industrial Democracy (SLID). The SLID in 1960 rebranded itself as Students for a Democratic Society (SDS)[7], because some of the new leadership of the time felt "Industrial" made them sound like they were more focused on labor and not on social issues. You see, these social justice warriors aren't like the ones you see online in memes, these were some rather frightful sons-of-bitches that have never been taken seriously in terms of political and cultural movements until recent years.

Without taking a position on whether they were explicitly pro-communists or a Marxist organization, they decided that they could be more effective at creating paranoia

[7] https://www.britannica.com/topic/Students-for-a-Democratic-Society

and strife by solely dedicating themselves to calling out what they opposed, instead of explaining what they were for. In a age of Democrats screaming "Russian collusion!" the progressives of the 20th century didn't mind standing next to the Soviets after the Kennedy assassination. SDS's goal was to call out the United States' "red scare" and positions towards the Soviet Union, claiming that any position taken against the Soviets was used as justification for trouncing privacy and civil liberties. The anti-communist Kennedy Democrats of the time who were involved with LID had always taken a clear stance that they were anti-communists, but the new manifesto chartered by SDS essentially claimed they would partner with any and every organization that would help them see their goals through. Long story short, tensions arose and LID broke ties with SDS in an effort to distance themselves from the Marxists and Soviet sympathizers that had now taken control over the student moving, turning into something that LID even feared as being too extreme for them.

SDS and its activists began to infiltrate the Democratic Party, going as far as to have some members take up roles in the 1964 Johnson campaign in order to advance their agenda. Others would join the growing Black Power movement of the sixties and get involved with the anti-war movement once the US got involved in the Vietnam conflict. A faction of SDS wanting to rebrand started an anti-war organization called Student Nonviolent Coordinating Committee (SNCC), which focused on civil rights issues at the time. This radical progressive student movement hit fever pitch during the free speech movement on the campus of the University of California, Berkeley, when activists led by student Mario Savio rioted, disrupted meetings, and blocked police movements in order to get their message across. As a result of Savio's protest, hundreds of students were arrested and the event brought international attention. This was the biggest achievement SNCC and SDS had achieved to date because they were officially mainstream.

In 1966, SDS activists began to riot and march on college campuses and even the Pentagon, with the aim of getting injured and arrested in order to cry victim. They claimed everything was done in order to protest the draft movement, bring attention to the women's liberation and Black Power movement, but inside of the SDS meetings, their ultimate goal was an anarchist revolution which would bring about a Marxist government implementing a communist regime.

In 1968, SDS anti-Vietnam protestors began a bloody riot outside the Democratic Party Nominating Convention in Chicago (are you noticing a trend in Chicago?) where tens of thousands of protesters and cops rocked the city and country while the event was televised for the world to see.

In 1969, a branch of the SDS turned into a violent, militant domestic terrorist organization known as Weather Underground[8], who killed cops, civilians, and bombed the Pentagon. Weather Underground leaders Bill Ayers (an Obama confidant later in life when Obama was a Chicago based community organizer), and his wife Bernardine

---

[8] https://www.britannica.com/topic/Weathermen

Dorhne, used every connection and loophole in the legal system to get away from their crimes, and now sit lavishly as professors at the University of Chicago while their victims' families never received justice. History is written by those who hold the pen, and the same progressive establishment which cherishes Ayers for his commitment to underserved and oppressed people tends to give deaf ears and selective amnesia to certain disturbing concepts such as, "kill all the rich people. Break up their cars and apartments. Bring the revolution home. Kill your parents, that's where the revolution's at," as Ayers said[9] during his domestic terrorist days. Those weren't just the words of a youth in revolt, that was the literal philosophy of the Weather Underground in Ayers' words.

In the mid 1970's SDS died out, and while a new SDS exists today thanks to the re-energized socialist movement brought on by Bernie Sanders, it is relatively obscure and unnoticeable. I bring this up to say that most of these SDS members probably didn't go to college to wind up blowing up buildings or getting beaten by cops, they were most likely just nice, regular people who these criminals lured into something greater.

Our postmodern world's philosophy, which came out of WWI, tries to instill in people the idea that there is no absolute truth, everything is subjective, the ends justify the means, there is nothing more to life than the material world, and that the solution to all of life's problems can be found in the coercive force of government. Postmodernism, also known as "cultural Marxism" which runs around under the guise of "political correctness" in most of today's headlines, is the tool of the progressive movement. Moses Apostaticus, a freelance writer with *The Daily Caller*, wrote in a 2016 op-ed titled *Cultural Marxism Is Destroying America*[10] that:

> Cultural Marxism is the Marxist dialectic fused with Freudian theory and applied to identity and culture. Like all forms of Marxism, it is based upon categorizing people into abstract groups and then creating a narrative of historical oppression between them. The strategy of Marxists is always to cultivate a victimized group and then convince its members that solidarity is required against the oppressors. This creates resentment and hatred and is how Marxist ideologies fulfill their revolutionary objectives.

Once you know what it looks like, you begin to see it everywhere; it was surrounding me in high school before it became the cancer on college campuses we know it as today, and it is how many people view the world who wouldn't even describe themselves as liberal or progressive. The goal of SDS was to permanently change how we see the world, and this manifest destiny was fulfilled in 2008 when newly elected President Barack Obama vowed to "fundamentally change" the United States. Obama was continuing what Ayres and SDS had started, but this time from the most powerful

---

[9] https://www.nationalreview.com/corner/bill-ayers-unrepentant-lying-terrorist-andrew-c-mccarthy/

[10] http://dailycaller.com/2016/09/29/cultural-marxism-is-destroying-america/

office in the world. You can't throw a rock at any leftist political institution, media outlet, or entertainment conglomerate and not hit an influential progressive either directly influenced or involved by this radical movement brought about by the plague known as SDS.

In 2008, as the Tea Party was beginning to get its groove on, several students who had never met one another and were on opposite ends of the country had an idea: what if they got their friends together and started a student group that stood up for free markets, individual liberty, and limited government? Yes, you had other student groups like that in terms of mission but the goals were entirely different. In order to play the game, you had to understand the game you were playing, and it seemed for decades that progressives and statists knew all along how the game was played while other right leaning organizations just kept to themselves.

In the aftermath of the Ron Paul 2008 presidential campaign, the National Youth Coordinator for Ron Paul, Jeff Frazee, looked at the activists and networks of students he had developed and understood it would be an absolute waste to let Dr. Paul's "revolution" as supporters were calling it, die because of a lack of vision. Frazee took the resources available and turned that network of student activists into a non-profit today known as Young Americans for Liberty (YAL). Almost serendipitous, in July of 2007, a group of students who had met at a Institute for Humane Studies Koch fellowship and developed a similar concept, this time creating an explicitly libertarian organization. The two students from that fateful summer who would go onto turn that idea into action were Alexander McCobin and Sloan Frost, who planned to operate a forty student conference which accidentally turned into over one-hundred students showing up at Columbia University in 2008, and from that day Students For Liberty (SFL) was born, sprawling into the largest libertarian student organization in the world.

Both SFL and YAL operate very similarly, especially since member crossover basically comes with the package of joining one or the other. From campus activism to conferences and activist boot camps, They took the community organizing model of recruit, engage, and activate to a new level sprouting thousands of campus chapters across North America alone. Without these organizations, the modern landscape of the liberty movement would easily die out.

SFL and YAL are staunchly different from SDS in one thing however, no matter how diverse the ideas and opinions of members may be, whereas SDS was willing to use violence, the libertarian and conservative students pledged to uphold the Non-Aggression Principle. The Non-Aggression Principle (or NAP as some call it) is the lynchpin of libertarianism, so to speak, and what separates freedom from tyranny. The NAP in its most basic definition can be broken down into the simple concept that you shouldn't hurt people or take their stuff just because you want to. If you think about it, through unjust wars abroad and civil asset forfeiture at home, the government along with a good chunk of Republicans and Democrats seem cool with breaking the NAP before lunch daily.

YAL and SFL have free speech balls and walls while SDS had bombings and murders. If you think indiscriminate murder and violence in order to implement your political ideology is cool, you should probably stop reading this book and walk into the ocean before someone gets hurt. It's kind of funny, millennials as a generation are stereotyped as ungrateful leeches on society, but it was their grandparents' generation in who rallied and protested for an ever expanding welfare state. Now, you have tens of thousands of conservative and libertarian young people who have in turn become the new counter culture against the progressive era of then President Barack Obama, forcing older progressives to try everything in their power to keep the concepts of classical liberalism and individualism far away.

Returning back to Marion Military Institute, I knew I had to keep this rush of excitement continuing and get others involved. By the end of the first month of the new semester, I already had the club paperwork approval signed and accepted by the administration and faculty sponsor willing to help out. For weeks following up to our first meeting, announcements, a Facebook page, and a flyers were all over campus. I was stoked for what the first meeting would look like. I was already just gliding on air, my student club, Marion Military Institute Student for Liberty (MMISL, pronounced like "missile") was recognized as the first libertarian student group in MMI history. The night of the first meeting, I spent $60 out of pocket on pizza, had the projector all set to show a few short videos, and tables full of free books and other SFL swag. I want to tell you it was the best night of my life and that it was full of people, but of the eighty or so students who who registered online or showed interest, only two showed up, and the dudes that were the Vice President and Secretary didn't even bother either.

It's disappointing. It takes out a chunk of your heart when you work hard to do something for the benefit of others and they don't show up. This wasn't the knitting club or something like that. Over the last year, I had heard from other students how it was strange a school that was supposed to pump out leaders in the public and private sector didn't have a political club of sorts. So imagine my surprise two people trying to consume $60 worth of pizza. In a way I thought this was going to be that student group back in high school, but what you begin to realize is that the rush of political excitement teens see, where it is red team vs blue team, goes away the older you get for many people because they have better things to do than care about politics. A good Republican friend of mine ran for Congress in Northern Virginia, and countless people promised to help him with his campaign, but it just ended up being him and his campaign manager knocking on doors collecting signatures; the establishment in Virginia called him a lost cause, and no one wants to work hard on a lost cause in their mind. A friend of mine who was running for House of Delegates booked an entire brewery and even brought in a food truck for his campaign announcement. Over 100 people confirmed but less than a dozen showed up. The last race I ever managed, I booked an event space for a town hall with my candidate, dozens of people confirmed but only one reporter showed up.

Imagine my surprise when I was the campus chairman for Students for Tom Garrett at Liberty University, and the only time we had all the volunteers we needed was when they got to meet the candidate when he came to speak on campus. Politics is a fickle point for people, everyone wants to be the candidate for office or big influencer on campus. No one just wants to get involved for the sake of being more knowledgeable. People want the glitz and glam with the stereotypical political scene, I've only really met a handful of people who were die hard, ground pounding activists.

Democrats will come out in waves for each other to promote their bad, destructive policies, but conservatives and libertarians won't show up to fight because they think they can't win. As bad as SDS was, no one can deny they were committed. The thing about politics is it is no different than anything else in life: sometimes you fight because the fight needs to be fought, not because you know you will win. People think it makes a loss worse when you give a fight your all and you still lose, but what no one realizes is that the act of fighting and willing to fight despite all odds is probably the biggest statement one can make in life. The godfather of American libertarianism, Barry Goldwater, lost badly in 1964 but it only took 16 years for us to get a President Ronald Reagan.

The next few weeks weren't any better. Doug Butzier died and I was in a boat without a paddle. Yes, I hoped having a US Senate candidate, a Libertarian nonetheless, speaking to my group would help drive interest, but having that person also be your friend and then die made everything far the more difficult. I cancelled the next month's worth of meetings, I was destroyed emotionally. I went a few days later to ask my faculty advisor if it would be in everyone's interest just to end MMISL altogether.

"Remso," he said, "what did you see in that room the other night?"

"Three people," I replied.

"Let's stick it out the rest of the semester. We have room for potential and we can make it work if you just give it a little more time." Potential for what? Most the people who showed up didn't even like libertarians or the ideas of libertarianism. One dude used to show up to try and convince me that George Bush was the best president ever and that the biggest problem in our country was that we weren't actually invading other nations and stealing "their shit" as he used to say. I began to think it was me, maybe I was too unpopular, or too argumentative, but that is when the thought hit me, the idea was "me." What if I took myself out of the equation? What if I could potentially fill the largest lecture hall in the school, which happened to be the upstairs of the library?

It just so happened I was reading a friend's copy of *Don't Hurt People and Don't Take Their Stuff: A Libertarian Manifesto* by Matt Kibbe, and towards the beginning of the book when discussing the Tea Party movement, he told the story of Becky Gerritson, the founder of the Wetumpka TEA (Taxed Enough Already) Party from Wetumpka, Alabama, who sat in front of Congressional committee regarding the IRS probing scandal involving the intentional targeting of conservative and libertarian organizations. During her opening testimony, Becky said something which would go down in Tea Party history:

> I am not here today as a serf or a vassal. I am not begging my lords for mercy. I am a born-free, American woman, wife, mother and citizen, and I'm telling my government that you have forgotten your place. It is not your responsibility to look out for my well-being or monitor my speech. It is not your right to assert an agenda. The posts you occupy exist to preserve American liberty. You have sworn to perform that duty, and you have faltered.

It hit me, Wetumpka was less than an hour away, and this woman was a conservative hero. Who better to talk about the ideas of liberty? I reached out to Becky and within a few days she agreed to come down. It was great. People were finally getting excited, even locals from the community wanted to come down and listen.

And this was when the problems started.

I was pulled into the Commandant of Cadets office five days before the event with Becky. I was nervous. It was never, ever a good thing to end up in his office.

"Cadet Martinez," an administrator was staring me from head to toe, examining every part of my uniform and my basically looking into my soul. "You know the upstairs lecture hall of the library can only be reserved for official campus organizations," he said. I was relieved, I actually always carried a copy of the club charter in my backpack. I told him we had been approved earlier this semester and all our paperwork was in order. He was a little baffled. Every other organization in the school was theoretically "cadet led," but the school official really made every decision and called the shots. Same went for all cadet leadership in the corps of around three hundred or so cadets. "I need to get this verified," he said. I was confused.

"Sir, I have the signatures from the Dean and the student activities director on that packet. Everything is in order," I said, but he looked at me as if I had taken a massive crap on his rug and rubbed it in with my boots.

"I need to verify this, then we'll see," he said in a tone which could only be interpreted to mean "get out of my office." I was starting to get nervous. We only had a few days left, but I couldn't pull back on promoting the event. I put flyers around campus, stamped with approval from the administration, and the next day they were all removed. I went to the cadet Battalion commander to ask what happened.

"We were told by the Commandant's office these weren't approved," he told me, I was pissed off severely.

"Sir, I have the stamp saying these flyers were approved." I showed him a flyer I had found in the trash with the stamp from the administration granting me permission. He just looked at me with a blank stare essentially saying go the fuck away. The final blow came the day before the event, the space was reserved and the food was ordered and the lecture hall was already arranged. I was called into the Commandant's office again, however.

"Cadet Martinez, your event can't be open to the public," the same administrator said in such a matter of fact way. I had followed all the rules, including the one that said because MMI was a public college, student groups can host events opened to the public if they are in the form of a public forum of sorts. "We don't want people to get the wrong idea from your politics and sorts." As if my club was advocating for pedophilia or reinstating slavery.

"Yes, sir," I said. There was no point in arguing, I couldn't afford to have this event canceled the day before it was all supposed to go down. The afternoon came and my small team of volunteers did what they typically did, not show up. So it was just my faculty sponsor and myself getting everything set up. "What do you think the potential for turnout is tonight?" I asked him.

"Hopefully more than three people. We have enough food for an army" he said.

We filled up the room. Becky brought her A-game, and it actually succeeded. People who never came to a meeting were laughing and talking about topics that my club was made for, and having Becky there as the expert and seasoned political veteran on hand made it so much better.

"What do you want to do, Remso?" Becky asked me before the event began that night.

"I actually don't know. I think I want to go be an intern for Matt Kibbe at FreedomWorks this summer though, see what it's like, I just got done reading his book."

"Let me make a phone call and let's see what we can do."

I felt like Alexander Hamilton leaving the Caribbean to go to New York, thanks to Becky's recommendation, I got to finally break into D.C.

Because I don't want to lead you on, there isn't anything driving this story into a happy ending or a suspense build up where you wonder "what happened to Remso's student group?" It died the semester I graduated. The school had given us mixed signals all year. The administrator who was always skeptical and the Dean of Students who was always supportive both gave a matching donation to a fundraiser we were doing, but on the day of a charity ruck march we did, they decided to take all the cadets who were assigned penalty hours and had them paint some dilapidated old building downtown and call them "volunteers" instead of "forced labor," and snag the reporter who was going to write a story about us. The school did that because our ruck march wasn't school sanctioned and you'd think a school that was supposed to mold and mentor young leaders would love the idea of cadets taking the initiative on a project. They didn't, and towards the end of the year they tried to make a power grab where they would forcibly take all our organization's donations and put it into an account we didn't have access to. At that point, asking permission to do what we wanted with our own money defeated the purpose of a libertarian club.

I look back and honestly, I was lucky all my group had to deal with was mild threats from the administration and a lack of respect. Other student groups have either been kicked off campus, censored, you name it. It has happened almost exclusively to conservative and libertarian student organizations. We need to be there for each other, we need to have each other's backs, even when the chips are down. Without cooperation, without innovation and the true disruptor mindset that drives social movements, nothing will work.

YAL, SFL, and Turning Point USA all put on countless conferences, connect students to expert speakers, put on mentorship programs and training seminars and throw awesome parties. These young and innovative organizations are winning because they don't let anyone stop them. They don't just bring students into the world of the liberty movement, but they mold them into becoming young professionals instead of the stereotypical neck bearded stoner libertarian youth are often painted with. As a member of the YAL Legacy Society, I get to be part of the first generation of libertarian student activists that get to pass the baton onward to those that will carry on the fight on college campuses across America tomorrow. Who knows, maybe one of these kids will be the next Ron Paul. Without backbone, nothing can be achieved. The youth are leading the revolution and now they are finally being noticed.

Chapter 7: The Economics of Hooters

"Without deviation from the norm, progress is not possible" ~Frank Zappa

Before I can take you to the swamp of D.C. I first have to take you to Nashville, Tennessee, about a month before I actually met Becky and managed to become a regular in the Commandant's office. Nashville is home to three very obvious things once you hit the main tourist area, a trolley with a fully functioning bar, a store selling cowboy boots on every corner, and so many bars with live music you'd lose count. The "Silk Road" and Bitcoin were buzzwords, ISIS was suddenly a threat, and Net Neutrality was right around the corner. If there was ever a more perfect place in the world to talk about sometimes scary, sometimes complicated, and sometimes exciting topics, Nashville is a good place to start.

There was an SFL conference going on at Vanderbilt University, and in order to be deemed a "real" chapter in the eyes of the SFL community, attending a conference was a big deal. Here was my pitch to the student body; I'll drive to and from, I'll cover the first meal, you get to hang out in downtown Nashville for an afternoon, and you get free food at the conference and a place to stay. I didn't even ask people to be remotely interested in SFL, I was hoping once they got there they would just get pulled into it somehow. I had over forty people sign up and managed to get a couple donations from faculty to cover food and gas. When push came to shove, only two of my friends showed up, which probably worked out for the best because at that point I was down to only one vehicle.

It was 4:30 AM the day we had to drive down, first we had to stop by the guard shack and sign out for the weekend. The security guard who checked our ID's and signatures asked us where we were going. "We're going to a Students For Liberty Regional Conference," I told him, he just scratched his head and looked at me.

"A what?" he asked.

"A libertarian conference," I said a little louder.

"One more time," he said, this time I was a little frustrated.

"Republican convention, we're Republicans," said Andrew, one of the two dudes who showed up to come.

"Oh I was in College Republicans too back in the day," the guard passed us back our drivers licenses.

"Good one, Andrew," I shoved him endearingly.

"We aren't going to a Republican convention?"

We were an hour onto the road and finally stopped at a Waffle House type of knock off near Selma. "Where are you boys heading so early in the day?" the waitress asked while pouring us coffee.

"We're going to a libertarian student conference ma'am" I said. She looked at me like I said a Nazi clambake, and finished pouring our coffee and shuttled away. Andrew and Rob (the other guy) both started laughing at me. "What?"

"Dude," Rob said but kept laughing, "you said lesbian student conference instead of libertarian." My blood went cold. I was dead tired a second ago but as soon as he said that I could see our waiter on the other side of the restaurant talking to the cashier and pointing at us. The day kept going, we had met up with the SFL chapter out of the University of Alabama at Birmingham who sponsored my group's attendance (since we were so small and in a unique circumstance having been at a military college). Later in the day we got to Nashville. As we were within a mile of our hotel, I saw restaurants the three of us hadn't seen in months thanks to being stuck an hour south of nowhere. Hyatt, Hilton, the row of hotels were awesome, we were so excited.

Imagine our surprise when we pulled up to the hotel that was being covered for us, and as we looked around the dilapidated shithole the only thought going through our heads were that this is where hookers go to die. The only upside was that it was across the street from a Hooters. After spending months in the middle of nowhere Alabama, the smell of the waitress's perfume and chicken wings basically turned us from respectable young military school men into mindless, intoxicated animals as we found every excuse to go off on our own and over to Hooters. Hooters is a human achievement and probably one of the purest examples of free markets, allow me to explain...

Economics, or the "dismal science" as some call it, comes to life in new and exciting ways when you really understand the peer to peer interactions that occur voluntarily without the presence of government. Hooters is one of those examples, where attractive women serve hot wings and beer to men (and families) in a fun and laid back environment. Someone once mentioned that countries that have a presence of McDonald's franchises will never go to war with each other. I would like to take it a step further and say that nations that have Hooters understand freedom a bit more than those who don't. Now, as a Liberty University alumnus, I get a lot of crap for being a proud Hooters customer. In my senior year of high school, you could often catch me and my buddies at the neighborhood Hooters on a Friday night, and every so often I'll still swing by after a day at the range for some wings and a whiskey with Coke. Many of my peers say Hooters exploits women, my response to that- absolute nonsense.

To exploit a person means there is an absence of choice and that an individual is being used without their consent nor allowed to keep the fruits of their labor. These women don't need to work at Hooters, they choose to work there. Yes, men don't go there for the wings alone, but that isn't something to be ashamed of either. Men like to watch beautiful women and be treated nicely, Hooters is essentially Chick-Fil-A but with more cleavage. Go to the bar at a Hooters, you'll find interesting and fun conversation, if you're single, perhaps some dating tips from women that know what they want in a man because they are confident in themselves and their standards. God knows if a restaurant called Banana Hammocks opened up and had men who dressed up as the Village People serve bottomless Mimosas to middle aged housewives, no one would scream "sexism" because our society still treats women like they can't make choices. I like to think the suffragettes are looking down from Heaven thinking "We won girls, we won" but maybe that's a stretch. Only in a free country where tolerance and innovation are allowed to flourish can human achievements like Hooters exist. Father of the Austrian School of economics, Ludwig Von Mises, once said "Society has risen out of works for peace, the essence of society is peacemaking." If Hooters isn't the most spot on example of a peace promoting environment, I don't know what is.

Radio host Clay Travis in 2017 went on *CNN* with anchor Brooke Baldwin to discuss a recent controversy regarding something some *ESPN* host said and at one point Travis stated "I'm a First Amendment absolutist and believe in two things completely-the First Amendment and boobs." By the look of Baldwin's face, you would have thought he advocated for the reinstitution of slavery. Maybe it's because my "things you shouldn't say in public" meter broke a long time ago, but if a fact is a fact, there isn't any reason to be embarrassed. There is a undeniable link between free speech, private property, and the amounts of a woman's body she is willingly and legally allowed to show adding up to the level of individual liberty a society allows. This is why countries like Saudi Arabia, North Korea, and Turkey don't have Hooters, its because they have a very minimal level of respect for freedom. When I see a Hooters restaurant, I don't think of boobs, beer, and wings first, I think of it being a testament to the inherent rights of man to live and prosper in a civil society.

Back to reality, Rob looked at the YAL president from Birmingham, "Why do we only have two room keys between the five of us?" then suddenly we stopped paying attention to the Hooters waitress with the short brown hair waving to us from across the street and crashed back into reality

"The five of us are going to have to share a room. Apparently that's all our chapters were able to get covered for," she said, and we all became extremely quiet. It was so awkward, Andrew took a bed, Rob was on the floor, and the Birmingham YAL president and her fiancé took the other bed three feet away from couch I was sleeping on. And yes, there were roaches and strange human bodily fluid stains on all the sheets. This was a moment where I looked at my student activist career and really thought to myself, "wow, this is really shitty, I'd almost rather be back at school," but we persisted nonetheless.

The next day at the Vanderbilt campus, over a hundred students showed up. It was by far the most mixed group of people I had ever encountered in a single formal setting. There were attractive women in cocktail dresses and others in workout hoodies. There were guys who looked they they walked out of a 1950's family sitcom with bowties, and dudes that stepped out of a goth album cover with so many piercings you'd lose track. There was a short dude probably in his fifties from Iraq who lectured us all on colonialism and a guy who looked like the unabomber wearing a *InfoWars* t-shirt and a Libertarian Party baseball cap. This was such an odd grouping of individuals, it didn't even feel strange, it just felt more interesting, in a good way. Where else will you get an eclectic group of people in a room like this outside of a Wes Anderson film?

In the exhibitor hall were representatives from a wide gamut of organizations ranging from Tea Party Patriots to NORML (National Organization for the Reform of Marijuana Laws), and in one corner was a booth for the Libertarian Party of Tennessee. At this point in life meeting another member of the Libertarian Party was almost like meeting a unicorn. A few weeks after Cato in California, I paid my dues to become a member of the Libertarian Party, and around that point my younger brother Ryan back home had become a volunteer for the Robert Sarvis for US Senate campaign. Robert is the smartest guy in the room anywhere he goes. The Libertarian Party post 2012 had begun to pick up so real steam since it seemed Gary Johnson was more popular after the election than he was before. A former candidate for Virginia State Senate as a Republican several years prior, Sarvis began to separate himself from the social conservative side of the party that was off putting to a large section of the population. Also still rejecting the economic illiteracy of the Democrats, Sarvis was always strong in his libertarian beliefs, and in 2013 switched from Republican to Libertarian in order to run for statewide office. Sarvis's record and ability to run a professional and model campaign made him stick out as a third party candidate, and thanks to his lasting contribution to the realm of libertarian policy influence in Virginia and 3rd party achievements, Ryan and I have been thankful to not only call him a role model and mentor, but also a good friend.

The Libertarian candidate running for governor of Tennessee was no Robert Sarvis however. In fact this guy from Tennessee managed to just piss me off.

All I wanted to ask what what it was like being a Libertarian and actually try and run for office. "It's kinda boring" he told me, "I mean I'm on the ballot so what else can I do at this point?" That irritated me so much. A few weeks prior my brother was with a few other volunteers outside of a gun show in Chantilly. Candidates and campaigns are allowed to pass out fliers and literature to folks walking into the convention center. Republicans have done it for years, and Ryan and his volunteers followed the exact same rules when working on behalf of the Sarvis campaign. Still, someone had an issue and decided to throw a fit and try and get them kicked out for some reason or another.

"The event coordinator needs to talk to you, there's been a complaint" the officer told Ryan. What could it be? A missing permit? Nope, Ryan walked in escorted by a bunch of angry, old Republicans over to the coordinator booth. This slimy, bearded man in desperate need of a shower stood up.

"You're not real libertarians!" he yelled at my brother, "You're not real libertarians or else you wouldn't be going up against a Republican!" and that is when it hit him, his was entirely politically motivated. Republicans who love their guns and free speech were intimidated by a kid and several volunteers advocating for a pro-free speech, pro-gun candidate, even less than a year after the election where conservatives across the country complained about the Republican Party failing them.

Lets back it up and cover one thing first, why did he accuse my brother of not being a real libertarian? And Why didn't I capitalize the "L" in "libertarian" even though I capitalized the "R" in Republican?

Things are about to get tricky...

Typically this is how the world operates- liberals and progressives are Democrats, conservatives are Republicans, moderates are Independents (revisit blender metaphor), but not all libertarians are Libertarians. Let me write that out again, not all libertarians are Libertarians. I know this must sound like I'm saying not all gays like dudes and not all vegetarians actually eat vegetables only. The Libertarian Party doesn't have a monopoly on libertarians actually being members. In fact, you should never assume you know what party a libertarian is affiliated with.

First, some libertarians are members of the Libertarian Party which should be a very obvious general assumption. Secondly, because of the history between libertarians and conservatives going back to the Goldwater era, many libertarians such as Rand Paul and Justin Amash have stuck with influencing the Republican Party. "But Remso, there is no point in trying to influence the Republican Party!" you might be saying, and in that case you are incredibly wrong and should stop interrupting yourself reading. That is rude to both you and me.

The age old debate of whether a libertarian should take over the Republican Party is well, an old one which no one can come to a conclusion on. Members of the Libertarian Party are considered "Big L" libertarians and libertarians not part of the Libertarian Party are called "Small l" libertarians, or as some members of the Libertarian National Committee have called them in the past, "fucking turncoats." "Small l" libertarians have been trying to take hold of the Republican Party since Barry Goldwater received the GOP nomination for president in 1964. This was at a time in GOP when many Republicans asked whether or not the GOP was a conservative party or just a watered down Democratic Party (sounds like today sometimes right?) Goldwater's bringing together of economic libertarians, anti-communists, and traditional conservatives is what paved the way for Ronald Reagan in 1980, but it also gave inspiration for the birth of the Libertarian Party in 1971 which was, you guessed it, named after the premise of being solely based off libertarian solutions.

In 1972, the Libertarian Party would earn its only Electoral College delegate thus far for a presidential nominee, a faithless Republican elector named Roger Macbride, who essentially got sick of everyone on both sides of the aisle screwing up the country so he cast his Electoral College vote for Libertarian presidential candidate John Hospers and vice presidential candidate Toni Nathan (also the first woman to receive an electoral college vote). Years later, Macbride himself would become the Libertarian nominee for president, and after several decades of dealing with institutionalized prejudice from the establishment parties and non-stop pandemonium from within the Libertarian Party itself, Macbride would get together with a group of libertarian-Republicans to form the

Republican Liberty Caucus[11], whose aim it is to push the GOP in a more libertarian direction by working within the party structure.

In my time as a student activist, community organizer, and political operative, I had always met more libertarians who were Republicans than libertarians who were Libertarian Party members. At the time of the Nashville SFL convention, I just assumed it was utter heresy to be a libertarian and a member of the two establishment parties. Rand Paul was great but too socially conservative, Ted Cruz was cool but nobody anticipated he would go on to pull half the things he did, and Justin Amash was just a junior congressman. The hostile takeover of the GOP, as many felt, died when Ron Paul was unable to receive the GOP nomination in 2012. To be a libertarian and a Democrat? The closest thought of that ever happening probably died when RFK was shot.

Sitting down with the Libertarian gubernatorial candidate from Tennessee, I just grew irritated. Here was my brother in Virginia being chastised for being a politically involved young person advocating for the principles of liberty while working for a candidate who was giving it his all on behalf of a thankless minor party, and I was sitting next to a dude that wasn't even trying. Andrew, sitting beside me leaned over to whisper something in my ear.

"I want to go to Hooters, please can we go to Hooters," he begged. We tried to leave the conference to go, but we quickly realized we had no car. We were stuck between a dude with a surplus of lip piercings and a dude that looked like the Unabomber. Cato University this was not, Hooters it wasn't either.

---

[11] http://rlc.org/history-rlc

Chapter 8: 3:10 to Selma

"Black people don't have to be Democrats."
~Chance the Rapper

Sometimes we have to really see and feel something to believe it. A common question I ask classes when I do online or in-person seminars about grassroots activism or podcasting, is whether or not they would rather go to Paris in person for a full week and pay for that trip out of their own pocket, or volunteer a willing friend to go to Paris where they pay out of their own pocket, and come back to report to you their experience. Either way, you will know more about life and culture in Paris now then you will have before. The key factor though isn't simply knowing more information and spitting out answers like you would have memorized for a multiple choice exam, the key is the experience that allows you a 360 degree view of the situation, the difference between being Dr. Jones the classroom professor, and Indiana Jones the adventuring archeologist badass.

At an activist summit in Cincinnati put on by FreedomWorks in 2016, a group of conservative and libertarian young people and I were put into a focus group for several hours simply about how to better message these liberty ideas to politically apathetic individuals along with those left-of-center folks who could still be saved before they began to think Venezuela was a good economic model for the US. There were two different sides it seemed: the side of preppy, upper middle class conservatives (the ones most likely to get drunk at College Republican functions) who essentially wanted to steal every Democrat social media strategy known to man and just stick their names on it, and the grungy libertarians which consisted of me (at the time a very unsuccessful community organizer and raging blogger who maybe had a dozen followers), a Libertarian running for California State Assembly named John Hoop, and a handful of others who dared ask the question as to why millennials and independents as a collective didn't care about our message to begin with.

Long story short, the night didn't go very well and names such as "sellouts" and "potheads" were thrown around the room interchangeably. We just didn't get along because the fundamental flaw I found in the conservatives was that they didn't seem to care about what their target audience cared about- the target "avatar" (hypothetical individual to whom we are targeting our solutions) being a young, college-aged ethnic/racial minority from a lower class background. None of the conservative solutions had anything to do with building bridges so that person could come across, instead their solutions could be described more as baiting someone over and maybe at some point they'll care to stick around.

"More memes!" Said the blonde haired fellow with blue eyes. "Show videos with more minorities," said the brunette who looked like your stereotypical southern belle. What the Hell does that have to do with anything? The problem conservatives don't seem

67

to grasp even at the time I am writing this is that they have a disconnect between tools and message.

Think of two soldiers from two battling armies with the same gear and the same weaponry. Who will win in a fight? Aren't they exactly the same because they are using the same tools of war? What is the problem with this question? You can't answer it because you don't know the reasons they are fighting, like who started it and the stakes at play. It's difficult and you'll never have all the facts needed to give an accurate answer, but most political debates regarding methodology are set up with inherent flaws, lack of information, and open ended outcomes. The right answer is the least obvious, the soldier with the better strategy is the soldier who will win, the weapons have really nothing to do with it at all because knowing how to fight is better than knowing that pulling a trigger shoots a bullet meant to kill. Now the soldier with no strategy but with more bombs and bullets, he'll lose every single time because the soldier that understands his weapons, gear, and how to effectively maneuver around the environment will win even if he has less at his disposal because it isn't about how much of something you have, it all depends on how you use it.

The issue isn't how flashy the pitch, the issue is the person selling it. Libertarian solutions about free market and crushing the welfare state don't fly in the inner city, and if you don't believe me please go stand outside a welfare line in NYC or Detroit or anywhere else and try quoting *Man, Economy, and State* and see how many converts you're able to pull. A fun sign that says "taxation is theft" won't work there either because your tax money is their food money. It is intellectually dishonest to say that race issues are entirely separate from politics, but this is something that conservative Republicans often try to deny. The problem is a kid from the streets of Selma or Oakland who lives in abject poverty day to day is not going to trust a well off white kid wearing a suit discussing the beauty of the invisible hand of the market.

Progressive Democrats get this wrong too. However, they think that race is permanently tied to identity politics, and if you are to encounter a conservative black man, he has to be a self-hating individual ashamed of his race. In a 2013 *Washington Times* op-ed titled *The Race-Hustlers Among Us*[12] by economist Dr. Thomas Sowell (someone who has been called every racially charged word under the sun including "Uncle Tom"), Sowell explained the differences between the asian population and their exceedingly high standards for life and academics, and the strikingly low aspirations of black Americans. Sowell mentions a lack of "leaders", stating:

> Some people try to explain why Asians and Asian-Americans succeed so well in education and in the economy by some special characteristics that they have. That may be true, but their success may also be a result of what they do not

[12] https://www.washingtontimes.com/news/2013/oct/22/sowell-the-race-hustlers-among-us/

have; namely, "leaders" who tell them that the deck is so stacked against them that they cannot rise, or at least not without depending on "leaders."

Sowell mentions the likes of Al Sharpton and Jesse Jackson, hypocrites who claimed to even be pro-life, anti-abortion advocates when the numbers regarding the thousands of black Americans who were killed as a result of abortion began to come out in the 1980's, all until the Democrats bought them off one by one to change their stance to match the Planned Parenthood agenda protected by the Democratic Party. Sowell used the tale of a Jewish fisherman with low aspirations as well, ending his article with "no one can claim that there was no anti-Semitism in America, any more than they can claim that there was never any anti-Asian discrimination. There was plenty of both. But that is very different from following 'leaders' whose message would only keep them grounded, after the skies were open to them as never before."

Republicans haven't helped themselves though, and have often ignored the plight of many lower income communities of color. A prime example of this is seen by comparing the Alabama GOP statewide victories of 2014 to the brutal beating they received in 2017 when Democrat Doug Jones defeated Republican Judge Roy Moore and became the first Democrat in decades to represent Alabama in the US Senate. Going back a little further, Alabama Republicans virtually destroyed the very infrastructure of the Democratic Party in Alabama during the sweeping GOP takeover of the nation during the 2014 midterms. The GOP in the state hosted a massive victory dinner to celebrate their success, and let me tell you, it was one of the strangest events of my life.

There was only thing in the world that would make me spend a ton of money on a ticket to go to a function put on by a political party I wasn't even part of, you guessed it, Senator Rand Paul of Kentucky. According to *Time Magazine*, Paul was "the Most Interesting Man In The Senate" and *Reason* called him "The Most Interesting Man In Politics" as well. For young libertarians around the country, Rand Paul was part Gandhi, part Elvis, and everyone knew he wanted to be president in 2016, it was a giant and open secret that only far and few between didn't know about. It seemed the libertarian moment many of us were waiting for was finally here ready to come down with the speed and force of Thor's hammer on the face of big government and injustice. Rand was invited to come speak at the Alabama GOP Victory dinner, and I found enough pocket change to purchase a ticket to go.

I drove three hours to Montgomery from Marion, I was so excited. Because I was still in school, I was able to get a pass to go with other students to actually meet Senator Paul. The meet and greet was rushed, but it was enough to keep me eager to hear his speech to the Republican attendees at the formal dinner that night. I walked around the hotel lobby where several PACs, organizations, and campaigns set up tables. An older gentleman ran over to me, and I got worried this senior citizen was going to attack me but the exact opposite happened. He grabbed me by the shoulder and shook my hand.

"I've been saying for years we need more hispanics in the party!" He yelled out with a giant smile on his face, looking at me as if he was a child seeing Santa for the first time at the mall.

"What the heck…" I said to myself while continuing to put on a rather fake and obviously uncomfortable smile. I brushed it off as he went away, probably to go hug the only black person who attended. The thing about Republicans is that Republican women are by far the most attractive, and as a recently single young man who'd been stuck in a confined military campus for five weeks with women who essentially looked and behaved like men, my intentions went more from waiting around for Rand Paul's speech to waiting around to see how many phone numbers I could get out of the night. Quick answer, none, because each time I was about to walk over, someone got in my way. After the awkward old guy, I went over to a table for the Run Ben Run! Presidential draft campaign for Dr. Ben Carson.

"If we can just get the black vote we can finally win again!" the gentleman at the table told me. I will say this, of all the early presidential nominees and prospective nominees for the GOP race in 2015, the Ben Carson volunteers were perhaps the kindest bunch I had the pleasure of hanging around, but something about this gentleman bugged me. Focusing his entire argument on the concept that you need a black candidate in order to get black people to vote for him reminded me of the 2012 election when minorities were used as props by local GOP committees. The tactic I often saw was cart out the minorities, make sure the press sees them standing and smiling next to you, and then put them back wherever they came from. This is what bugged me about Republicans as much as it bugged me about Democrats, minorities were always props and never people, Republicans always jump on Democrats for identity politics, but when they do it everyone acts like the situation isn't awkward.

I saw this cute blonde in a red dress standing alone near a table full of drinks, and right before I went to go talk to her, this tall, rather large guy around my age came and put his arm around her. He was running for Chairman of the College Republicans of Alabama, and you would have thought from the number of people that ran over to shake his hand that he had either cured cancer or had some hidden millions somewhere in the hotel. He was like Andre the Giant, but southern. While I was wondering what a girl like that was doing with a dude like that, he looked at me and all of a sudden I heard "Remso?"

I realized that the president of the College Republicans (a group that started three months after mine in order to counter the "anarchist threat") at MMI had mentioned to him I'd be coming, and thanks to my name tag and terrible barracks haircut I kind of stuck out too.

"Everyone, Remso here is the president of ISIS," he said while directing the crowd's attention towards me.

"Actually it's MMISL, ISIS is a terrorist organization," I replied.

He came over and we started chatting, his questions and small talk were turning a little bit more confrontational and then I realized it, the dude back at school didn't just want this bozo to show me some good ol' Alabama hospitality. This was his opportunity to debate a libertarian. The obvious remarks were thrown out with the obvious loaded questions, "How can you be a fan of open borders? How can we do nothing in Syria? The gay agenda is destroying families," and they just kept coming and coming and coming. If high school taught me one thing it was don't dig your own grave, so I just stood there and politely either pivoted the conversation or tried to block his questions by one thing or another to prevent me from being seen as confrontational in a swarm of people who were far from being my friends.

While the term libertarian had become more widely used in the Republican Party, it was only really popular on the east coast and in the beltway thanks to Cato. Down south, saying you were a libertarian was essentially saying you were a Democrat who liked guns, some of the old guard GOP types saw us as no different than Obama, sadly.

The speech was about to start, the dude running for chairman came by and shook my hand and issued me a gentleman's goodbye. "Enjoy Senator Paul, he's one of your types." I still can't tell whether that was some underhanded remark or him just stating a fact. Establishment Republicans hate libertarians because libertarians within the GOP don't care about whether they need to go toe to toe with their own party. During Rand Paul's second term and Ted Cruz's first term, they were often fighting Republicans more so than Democrats. In Matt Kibbe's book *Hostile Takeover*, Kibbe mentions that "sometimes you have to beat the Republicans before you can beat the Democrats," which is something many forget. We'll come back to this point later on though, so keep it in the back of your mind.

I found my table and sat down, made small talk with the guests around me and eagerly sat at the edge of my seat waiting for Senator Paul to speak. He got on stage and I was hooked, he spoke about things no other Republican in the country spoke about. Paul spoke about equal justice under the law, the crony and disastrous war on drugs, police militarization, issues that Republicans at least in my time being politically aware never spoke or even cared about. He even went as far as to remind those in the room that mandatory minimum drug sentencing was an obvious racial issue that was destroying the black and latino communities. Sadly, as I looked around the room, his speech seemed to go in through one ear and out the other for many. For many establishment Republicans, the Republican Party has nothing to do with expanding liberty: it's all about a power grab and they want to be at the top of the pile.

Later, one of the spokespeople for the Alabama GOP came up after Dr. Paul's speech to go over the party's numerous accomplishments within the last election cycle, one of them being expanding minority outreach.

"If you're a minority in the room, will you please stand up so we can recognize you?" She said, about four black men stood up and they received thunderous applause. Now, maybe I'm just overly sensitive but I don't know how someone can ask for the "minorities" to stand up and you, as a minority, not get pissed. How awkward would it be if I was at an event and I asked "can all the white people please stand up?" You'd probably feel a little weirded out wouldn't you? The guy sitting next to me poked my shoulder.

"Come on man, stand up" he said, I was pissed. I wasn't upset with him though; he didn't mean it in any malicious or mocking way whatsoever. But this is what I have a problem with: Republicans that literally place people in the same blocks and categories as the Democrats do. What if maybe the Republican Party has a problem with minorities because they don't like being called minorities? I once saw a comedian bring up a topic similar and say something along the lines of "I don't wake up in the morning, look in the mirror and say to myself that I'm black."

Fast forward to 2018: Donald Trump is the President and Republicans have a majority throughout most state governments and the federal government. Judge Roy Moore, who seemed to have everything going for him election wise, was hit with scandal after scandal by the liberal media and Republicans alike, and ended up losing by a pretty heavy margin to Doug Jones. The Republicans will tell you it was because the establishment class hated him and the liberal media spread a bunch of fake news, but the numbers tell a different story. Black voter turnout was much higher for Doug Jones than it was for Hillary Clinton just two years back. The Republican Governor Bentley had been caught in an affair and didn't do anything to address unemployment and taxes that adversely affected the black and lower income bracket of citizens either. Black voters felt Roy Moore and Republicans didn't have their back, and because of that they were willing to go out and vote for Jones. Yes, the Roy Moore scandals and attacks did allow independents and third party candidates to jump in and take votes that would have probably gone Republican, but the Republican defeat had its stage set years prior, it didn't just start when Roy Moore decided to jump in the race.

The next day I made the trek back to Marion and the route I picked had me coming through the Edmund Pettus Bridge in Selma, the notorious bridge where Dr. King and his followers were brutally beaten and ravaged by police sent down by the governor of Alabama. Today you go by it and there are some plaques commemorating what happened. When you search the bridge online you'll see that and then the main part of town with businesses and museums. What you never see is what is on the other side of the bridge when entering or leaving Selma. The Selma Civil Rights Memorial sits next to a building long abandoned with broken glass everywhere. The memorial, which is a pile of stones stacked upon each other and then several other small granite monuments stand alone, is almost too easy to drive past regardless of your direction. When I pulled over to visit I noticed the trash everywhere, I honestly felt nervous walking around because used cigarettes and broken beer bottles were strewn over the lot.

There is a mural on the side of the building on the grounds of the memorial, it is vibrantly colored and Dr. King, the bridge, and the shadows of those that walked across it. What you also see is the face of Rev. James Reeb, the white, Unitarian pastor who was beaten to death when walking out of a restaurant the night of the march on the bridge by a crowd of white men with clubs. Whether by omission or ignorance, Rev. Reeb's killing is often never brought up in most public school teachings of the civil rights era because many radical progressives want to paint a picture that white men and women had no part in the civil rights movement. What's ironic is that Republicans have allowed Democrats to rewrite the history of the civil rights movement. What was funny was in 2012 when liberal commentators accusing Romney of wanting to take the civil rights movement back 50 years, but it was his father, senior statesman George Romney that marched publicly with blacks during the height of the civil rights movement. They also tend to ignore the contributions of non-Democratic progressives such as Bernie Sanders, who regardless of your opinion of him, was in fact an activist during that time as well.

What broke my heart about the sorry state of the memorial was that at a time of intense racial division spurred further by Obama's Justice Department and the rampantly abusive and growing police state and militarization we all had to witness during the riots in Ferguson, Missouri. This memorial to the brave men and women who sacrificed life and limb for the right to live and be protected equally under the law, would be allowed to just wither away into nothingness. Selma today was still a town where the Democrat government profited off of poverty and low expectations. Just like any major city ran by Democrats, Selma had and continues to have high crime and massive unemployment. The main issue I found talking to locals and just my own observations is that you can be free legally, but when you allow the system to dictate your life mentally and emotionally and choose to remain spiritually caged, what difference does it make?

Democrats have failed the black and Latino communities for a century already (most Asian-Americans haven't forgotten FDR's concentration camps either), but Republicans have failed over and over again to remedy the situation. I wish I could have taken all those rich Republicans from the night before to that memorial, let them see it, experience it, and look around that the decay as they turn to look at the city across the bridge and realize they lack of compassion and commitment has allowed more lives to wither away and more families fall astray. I wasn't a Republican at the time because I didn't think Republican policies weren't the right solutions, I wasn't because I didn't think they actually cared in the slightest what the least among us had to live like.

Selma, Detroit, Chicago, LA, Flint, Washington D.C. are all examples of the institutionalized failure that continues to live because of the monopoly of force Democrats have obtained through control of cities throughout our country. Some of the most hardcore libertarians I have ever encountered are blacks and other minorities,

73

because if you ever want to understand why government is never the source of your salvation, go straight to those that had to live under the reign of those that have continued to let the liberal plantation grow over the years. I think the main difference between conservatives and libertarians is that a conservative is a libertarian who just hasn't gotten mad enough yet.

When you look at the issue even deeper, Dr. Sowell is entirely correct in stating that the problems and solutions lay entirely at the feet of the individual. In a piece for the *Daily Caller*[13], my friend and role model Jennifer Grossman, CEO of the Atlas Society, wrote a piece about a black family who became inspired to reach their full human potential after reading the works of Ayn Rand, eventually passing on their inspiration to their grandson who is paving his own roads in the liberty community. Grossman wrote:

> The Robinsons cited *The Virtue of Selfishness* as the work by Rand which influenced them most. On the surface it seems an odd choice for a couple who were motivated to pursue graduate studies at Columbia University in New York with the express desire to return to their communities to make a difference... Fortunately, the youngest Leonard's [the grandson] experience with racism is rare. He recalls attending a rally for Rand Paul with a white friend who drove them to the event. Afterwards, as the two approached the friend's vehicle in the parking lot, a woman leapt out and accosted Leonard, who was walking few paces in front. "Why are you trying to break into this car?" she yelled, accusingly. Leonard recalls: "My friend rushed in and told her it was his car, and I was his friend. It wasn't till later I thought, 'Oh, so that's racism.' I guess I hadn't really experienced it before."

The article ends saying something I'll never forget, "In a society, and particularly during a month, where black pride is exalted, Peggy Robinson put the focus on 'self-pride'." Imagine if progressives didn't push the bigotry and soft-racism of lowered expectations and conservatives didn't simply try to simply convert more blacks so they could have a bigger team for appearances sake? One reason I'm a libertarian is because this was the only political philosophy that told me to be me, as corny as that sounds. Being a mixed race person in Obama's America alone, everyone tries to put you in one box or another at some point.

Within 24 hours of that trip from Montgomery to Selma, I saw two very different worlds of people that could have easily been ripped from the pages of *A Tale of Two Cities*. It took me having to experience what poverty looked and smelled like to understand that there is an entire segment of our country that is trapped in the lies of low expectations and institutionalized prejudice. If lovers of liberty want to have their message engage and empower those in impoverished and underserved communities, they

---

[13] http://dailycaller.com/2018/02/23/self-pride-vs-black-pride-how-ayn-rand-inspired-this-black-couple-to-triumph-over-adversity/

have to stop seeing it as a "poor problem" or a "black problem" or whatever and see it as a human problem. Until there is genuine sympathy in their words and true passion in their hearts, no amount of outreach will go anywhere and the word "liberty" will just sound like another pitch.

Chapter 9: No Saints in the System
"The systems not broken, there are good people here, the system has been poisoned"
~Congressman Tom Garrett

Many young people, all bright eyed and bushy tailed, make it to Washington D.C. and expect things to turn into a scene from *Mr. Smith Goes To Washington*, but what you get more of is *Ides of March*. My first D.C. internship at FreedomWorks was exhilarating: I got to go to fun parties and meet important people. You almost feel like you're on the pulse of the nation. To go to work, be part of a big project, and then see your bosses and co-workers on the news when you get home makes you feel incredibly important.

Spend enough time in D.C., however, and you begin to realize that you don't matter at all. The folks who run D.C. don't love you, in fact many of them despise "flyover" country ("flyover" is the typical term progressives use for middle America). Right wing provocateur Alex Jones, the 9/11 truther and man notorious for exposing the agenda to "turn the frigg'n frogs gay" (it's true by the way[14]) was another person I had been told to stay away from during my journey into the political scene, around my second year of college. "You sound like Alex Jones, Remso," people would say when I would simply bring up an inconvenient truth about someone's sacred cow. People need to seriously stop telling me to avoid things, it just makes me more curious (for the record, public school graduates, smoking one cigarette will not get you addicted either). Moving on, I honestly thought the whole Alex jones conspiracy porn network known as *InfoWars* was satire and people were making a bigger deal about Jones and his antics than there needed to be. How can you know what something is like if you've never been exposed? *Infowars* isn't cocaine or bear boxing. Watching an hour of his show won't kill you. It'll probably make you wonder if intergalactic vampires run the Federal Reserve at least and give you a migraine.

While Jones had been around for about twenty years, I first encountered his website around 2014, close to the time he began to pick up more traction during the Obama years but especially during the beginning of the Republican primaries getting ready for the 2016 election when *InfoWars* essentially became mainstream news after the Trump victory. Good, bad, or indifferent, whether you like him or hate him, to say that Alex Jones is wrong all the time isn't true. Don Lemon from *CNN* isn't wrong all the time either, or the reputation killing hit squad at the *Huffington Post* or *Vox*, and it pains me to say that. People writing Jones off as wrong on 100% of his reports is like me saying that about *MSNBC*. Liberal media is a lying, openly corrupt cesspool, but even a broken clock is right twice a day. It's just the way of the world.

When you work for the News Analysis Division for a major network, or as I did at the Media Research Center, you have to watch hours and hours of a network you're assigned to observe. Something you notice over time is that most of the news you see is

---

[14] https://www.dailywire.com/news/18204/contraceptive-pills-turning-freaking-fish-amanda-prestigiacomo

commentary. Fixed narratives and spin mixed with the newest talking points. Everyone just says the same thing over and over again. There is no real push or pull by the journalist. They treat guests like they are fighting in a underground toddler fight club where dads waiving cash around watch to see their kids fight each other. Imagine the toddlers are our reputation as a country and the dads are the media, the moms are probably wondering what the Hell is going on and where is everyone while walking around nervous and confused, home alone. We the people are the nervous and confused mom. The dad comes home and says the toddler just fell down some stairs. Yeah, obviously that black eye on the quiet kid wasn't from a trip down the stairs, and yes, that cash hanging out of the dad's back pocket is awfully suspicious since he's been unemployed for a while, but it's better for most people to believe a comfortable lie than an inconvenient truth. Still, the seeds of distrust once planted are hard to kill when they begin to sprout.

Where Jones finds his success is in the same area other media outlets find theirs: creating distrust where it might be and exploiting where it is. Turn between *InfoWars* and *CNN* long enough and while their talking points are drastically different, the paranoia and fear you begin to feel as you go down that rabbit hole grows as you go deeper and deeper. While you're in D.C. you think everyone has the nation's interest at heart, and you eventually realize that's not so black and white. Look at Alex Jones and Alex Jones' wannabes throughout Al Gore's amazing internet and you'll begin to think "maybe I can see where the anger is coming from."

Promoting massive distrust of American civil institutions isn't unique to Jones, but he's up there when it comes to those that know how to craft a narrative and feed it to his echo chamber in terms of an extreme example. If it sounds like I'm picking on *InfoWars* fans, I'm not in the slightest, it is better to be constantly suspicious of your government than not to. There is an episode of *That 70's Show* where Hyde, an orphaned hippie living with his best friend Eric's family, discusses the real three branches of government stating "the three branches of government are the military, corporations, and Hollywood." It's funny to have a liberal hippie from TV sitcom say such a libertarian-esque, anti-establishment statement, especially when you see the Hydes of yesterday in reality turn into the angry progressive college professors of today. Look at the news during a Republican administration and the Democrats want you to question all government action and resist the state. Look at the news during a Democrat administration and Republicans want you to question all government action and resist the state. See any difference? The truth is in D.C. there isn't a bucks difference between the two of them.

Where is this all going? Apart from Ronald Reagan and Calvin Coolidge who attempted to curb the excessive growth of the federal government, the last hundred years has been defined by the progressive era that started in the labor movements of the 19th century in Europe and seeped its way into our churches, unions, and governing institutions starting primarily with President Woodrow Wilson.

As the government grew, the interest in owning parts of it became even more lucrative as big business, bankers, and unions alike all tried to buy out whoever they could. This is how crony capitalism starts and why we have never had truly free markets, because private entities collude with insiders within the government and they cut deals to ensure everyone gets their way. When you think about it, a Bernie Sanders campaign speech is very similar to a Ron Paul speech, but the problem is between the lines. Bernie received millions from unions alone when he ran for president, he was in their pocket entirely and while he was almost correct in his analysis of crony capitalism, his remedy was more government. Paul on the other hand had the largest number of small sum donors out of any candidate in 2008 and 2012 when he ran. While Paul gives an analysis of crony capitalism almost similar to Bernie's, the difference is the solution, take away the incentive to control the means of power produced by the state.

I was the only one of the interns at FreedomWorks when I was there who actually wanted Ted Cruz to be president. Everyone else was a Rand Paul supporter. I never had any gripes or complaints about Rand Paul, but in terms of identifying the issues I felt Ted Cruz not only had the idea pinpointed but understood what needed to be done to win. Because of that I believe that is why it was down to him and Donald Trump at the end of the day for the GOP presidential nomination in 2016. Rand wanted to wage war on the "Washington Machine", Ted wanted to go after the "Washington Cartel." both terms sound almost synonymous, but they carry very different implications.

In order to understand the whole picture, let's break down the sad painting of a politician known as Rick Santorum, whom most of America forgets ran for president a second time in 2016 (never Google "Santorum" without first adding "Rick"). Santorum was a rather popular senator from Pennsylvania as some of you may remember, and somewhere down the road he lost an election and decided it was time to run for president. Things looked good for him for a while. He was your very stereotypical Mr. Republican figure, sweater vest and all. He picked up endorsements in 2012 from the likes of Glenn Beck and Michelle Malkin during the primaries, but faltered when it came to gather the delegates needed to get the nomination. 2016 wasn't any better. Most Americans didn't know he was running. Mr. Republican spent most of the time attacking and complaining about Rand Paul and Ted Cruz, but no one cared to notice.

During a lecture at the University of Chicago School of Politics in 2013[15], around the time of the rise of liberty Republicans such as Rand, Ted, Mike Lee, Justin Amash, and Thomas Massie, the sad and forgotten Rick Santorum decided to go after libertarians calling them a "fad." Santorum continued his lecture saying "libertarianism is foundationally flawed in its thinking... one is society is based upon the individual, and that America is based all upon rugged individualism. That's not what America is about, the basic unit of society is the family, not the individual." First thing's first, Santorum is wrong and he is right, but it is more of a chicken or an egg scenario as in what came first,

---

[15] https://www.youtube.com/watch?v=e6LGfTtWGeg

the individual or the family? Scientists, sociologists, you name the specialty and everyone agrees you will struggle to find strong individuals where you lack strong families, and vice versa. Santorum picking a flaw with this is really nothing but a false dilemma, and when he continued to say "the family is the foundation from which all individuals come" he isn't wrong, but I can continue to go ahead and ask where did the family come from? Are they not a family tied together by the beliefs and character of the head of the house? One individual who maintains the peace, pays the bill, and keeps the family affairs in order? Chicken or the egg, family or the individual, both are just as important regardless of what you claim comes first.

Santorum continues, saying, "I look at policy through the eyes of how it affects the family," which is what all politicians say, right? Doesn't everyone want to look out for grandma and little Timmy? When you say you are doing something in order to benefit families, anything becomes doable and justified. You can do anything under the sun and say all your opposition is anti-family for simply opposing you. "Secondly, libertarianism is based on a flawed understanding of the nature of man. The idea that the people should go out and do whatever they do and if we just get government out of everyone else's lives everything will be fine... The idea that if men and women left to their own design everything will be great is a very flawed view of humanity." Right there, Santorum has just ignored hundreds of years of classical liberal philosophy (for which libertarianism is based upon). Libertarians never, nor has any classical liberal thought leader ever claimed, that man is inherently good left to his own design. Most classical liberal thought follows a Christian worldview which claims man is inherently flawed because of Original Sin.

While the moral crusader, Santorum, paints libertarians with a secular brush, he ignores the hundreds of Christian thought leaders such as John Locke, the father of natural law theory and western liberalism. Locke understood the flaws of man, which is why in his natural law theory he explicitly discusses the right to self defense and private property. Santorum paints the picture that without the coercive force of government, all of civilization would fall into a *Mad Max* type of situation, with nuns filming porn and children smoking meth outside of the local convenience store watching a homeless guy get stabbed to death. What many political scientists and historians hardly accept or admit is that the concept of tolerance and respect for individual rights in the western sense came from the Protestant reformation, not out of the secular age of enlightenment.

I had a professor at Liberty University who is among one of the smartest men I ever met, but there was always this one thing about him that bugged the Hell out of me. He could recite Friedman and Hayek and Mises by heart, but he had a stiff moral opposition to libertarianism. He cited Adam Smith's *Wealth of Nations* stating that because libertarians absolutized the marketplace above all other things, this left no room for God or moral beings. However, he knowingly never mentioned Smith's other book to the class, *the Theory of Moral Sentiments* that showed only a just and moral society could truly allow society to flourish and prosper. It was Smith himself who said "virtue is excellence, something uncommonly great and beautiful, which rises far above what is vulgar and ordinary" along with "man naturally desires, not to be loved, but to be lovely." Smith understood quite clearly that to be a good and ethical person had to be a choice, but it was also the best choice.

Continuing, Santorum says something I actually agree with, that "we need laws and institutions to shape and mold people to do the moral and right and ethical thing- the family, churches, community organizations. And part of that is laws, that teach as well as prescribe and govern." Santorum is right, we need those institutions such as churches and the family to build strong individuals, but with that statement he contradicts himself because these institutions are made up of individuals who didn't have to be coerced by the state to come together. He also insinuated that libertarianism is another term for anarchism which teaches no government at all. Even then, lets play along and say he is explicitly discussing anarchism (or anarcho-capitalism). Has there ever been a point in human history where the state or social institutions didn't appear in a power vacuum?

The speech goes on but essentially Santorum states that government as a function is inherently good and those dastardly, immoral libertarians want to host gay weddings with free weed in front of a Planned Parenthood clinic. In Santorum's world, everything is awesome and you don't have to worry about the big bad government unless you are doing something he doesn't like. In his 2016 presidential campaign, Santorum had a catchy slogan of his own saying he could "defeat the Clinton machine." Santorum was quick to target Hillary Clinton, and for good reason, but at the end of the day they were essentially the same. They both advocated neoconservative policies and dangerous domestic economic policies such as increases in the minimum wage, they were essentially the only candidates that supported the Export-Import Bank, and they wanted to double down on the war on drugs. Essentially, Santorum's ideal government is good as long as the right people (him ultimately) are in charge.

The "Clinton Machine", the "Washington Machine", and the "Washington Cartel" are very different things and the space between them tells the story. While the "Clinton Machine" implies everything is good as long as she isn't in charge, you go deeper and it simply is designed just to target one person, not a systemic issue that virtually all Americans know exists within the inner workings of our government. Rand's "Washington Machine" and Ted's "Washington Cartel" are more similar though. In his speech declaring his presidential campaign, Rand took aim at the expanding and intrusive federal government that was nurtured into existence by Republicans and Democrats alike. Paul at the podium proclaimed "the Washington Machine that gobbles up our freedoms and invades every nook and cranny of our lives must be stopped! Both political parties and the entire political system are to blame." Senator Paul has always said he wanted a federal government so small, it could at least "fit in the Constitution." A proven fighter and patriot, Senator Paul's assessment of the state of our government is true. However, going deeper always fleshes out the bigger issues. Santorum didn't want you to trust

Clinton, Rand Paul doesn't want you to trust big government, but what about Ted's cartel?

A "cartel" defined in the Merriam-Webster dictionary is "a coalition or cooperative arrangement between political parties intended to promote a mutual interest." You might read that definition and think by "political parties" they are simply talking about Democrats and Republicans, but it goes deeper. Politics by definition is "the activities associated with the governance of a country or other area, especially the debate or conflict among individuals or parties having or hoping to achieve power." Yup, everyone is at some point making a political play for power. The issue Santorum doesn't understand isn't that libertarians have no trust in government or everyone else at face value, its that they don't have faith in politically driven individuals to act in good faith when they demand a bigger gun for your protection, then point it at you. Libertarians fear a monopoly of power because they understand that man is flawed and it is far too dangerous to give anyone the power of life and death without restraint.

After dropping a verbal nuke on the Senate floor for calling out Majority Leader Mitch McConnell's lies regarding the secret Republican plan to reauthorize the Export-Import Bank (which is essentially a bank that gives your tax money to corporations and big business) in 2015, Cruz took time to speak to Rush Limbaugh on air to define the true nature of the Washington Cartel. Cruz stated "its career politicians in both parties who get in bed with lobbyists and special interests...we [Republicans] funded Obamacare and Obama's executive amnesty and Republican leadership jammed through the confirmation of Obama's Attorney General Loretta Lynch… the answer is the lobbyists and special interests and giant corporations that want big government and power give campaign contributions to both Republicans and Democrats." Cruz was able to drag vampires into the light on this issue by not only pointing out the fatal flaws of big government but also what happens when those with political clout use their resources to seize more of it.

You see folks on the left and the right protesting one thing or another but the problem at the end of the day is we are still stuck in the same messed up left-right spectrum of thinking where business has to be evil and government is entirely good or business is good and government is entirely evil. When you look at those inside our government who are giving away our freedoms and tax money in exchange for more power, it makes you not only take a side but sadly shed some honest and hard truths on those you may have thought were on your team.

Ted Cruz was the only Republican to stump in Iowa during the campaign and say to a crowd full of farmers that he would eliminate ethanol subsidies. It isn't a sexy issue, but how is it some Republicans cry out against picking winners and losers when Democrats do it but end up providing money for corn farmers and money for bombs from defense contractors we don't really need? There is too much blind faith in the same argument Rick Santorum makes, we just need the right people in charge and everything will be alright.

Professor of Economics at George Mason University, James Buchanan, developed a theory which simplifies the answer to this problem. "Public Choice Theory" as its called, is often referred to as "politics without romance" or as William Shughart II who in the *Concise Encyclopedia of Economics*[16] puts it:

> The wishful thinking it displaced presumes that participants in the political sphere aspire to promote the common good. In the conventional "public interest" view, public officials are portrayed as benevolent "public servants" who faithfully carry out the "will of the people." In tending to the public's business, voters, politicians, and policymakers are supposed somehow to rise above their own parochial concerns.

Long story short, those in the government and the politicians that run things aren't any better than anyone else, or else we wouldn't have a scandal regarding selling secrets or secret mistresses every other week on the news. Doesn't matter however, progressive indoctrination in our public schools has established the mindset that the ultimate good comes from the state and that one day we will progress into a world with a cradle to grave nanny state. Despite this knowledge we may all want in our wildest dreams live in Rick Santorum's sweater vest paradise, or even Hillary Clinton's *Hunger Games* paradise, where the size of government doesn't matter as long as the right people are in charge, just pick your poison. It is so much easier to believe that the people who are in charge of you, love you than it is to realize that a good number of them would wipe you off the face of the Earth if they couldn't find a way for you to line their pockets.

This is where the cartel has us trapped, the military industrial complex alone acts as a branch of government dividing power between the defense industry and the state. President Eisenhower warned us that "in the councils of government, we must guard against the acquisition of unwarranted influence, whether sought or unsought, by the military industrial complex. The potential for the disastrous rise of misplaced power exists, and will persist." The media and the political parties are another incestuous situation, and the list goes on from the pharmaceutical industry to what Congressman Tom Garrett of Virginia calls "the educational industrial complex" that exists between the web connecting our own Department of Education to the Bill and Melinda Gates Foundation (who birthed Common Core) and the other companies that move people around between their offices and the Department of Education interchangeably. This is cronyism pure and simple which free markets and a firm separation between lobbyists and government officials could cure if the rules were respected and enforced justly, not just when someone needs a political opponent knocked out.

Obamacare was one of the biggest financial rackets in our nation's history; it was collusion between the federal government and the wealthy elites to guarantee a massive

[16] http://www.econlib.org/library/Enc/PublicChoice.html

payday for insurance companies. Obama said more people would be covered and that quality of care would improve but that proved to be a massive farce. The federal government became the henchmen for the insurance companies and if you didn't purchase your Obamacare plan, the fines would hit you right where it hurt- your wallet. For a man who pledged to fight cronyism and Wall Street, Obama opened the door wide open for them to come in and dictate public policy from everything ranging from energy to agriculture.

This is one reason why I argue with Alex Jones fans who believe in the most elaborate of conspiracies involving our government, because most the problems going on aren't even conspiracies, they are open truths you and everyone can see with your own two eyes that people willingly choose to ignore because of the political and social repercussions that come with calling them out. Besides, the people they accuse of controlling the weather couldn't even get the Obamacare website to function, they aren't that smart to collaborate on century long and super detailed conspiracies. With all that said though, what I'm trying to get across is at some point, people need to seriously question the institutions around them regardless as to whether or not they'll face some type of persecution by those that don't want to rock the boat. Libertarians complicate their fears regarding massive centralized power and unjust authority, it is simpler just to point out the massive corruption and issues going on in front of everyone and taking things from there towards finding the root of the issue, which in essence is the role we have placed on the state to have as much authority as it has.

The cartel continues to live and thrive while hiding in plain site, and that's the worst thing about it. The threats of the police state, unending foreign wars, attacks on our civil liberties and our bastardized monetary system used to be seen as conspiracies and myths, but now are part of our daily conversation. The choice to be of the libertarian persuasion is a blessing and a curse because you'll never be surprised when something bad happens but you're always on your guard. Regular people like the ones I grew up with sadly find themselves slaves to the omnipotent and omnipresent state because they refuse to even question it's very capabilities. To regular, politically apathetic people, start questioning too much and you sound like Alex Jones screaming about the gay frogs (seriously, go research the gay frogs, that stuff is legit).

There are good people in Washington trying to do the right thing, but they are in the slim minority. During the first year of the Trump administration, we saw the House Freedom Caucus go toe to toe with the Trump administration and elected Republicans and Democrats alike because they understood that passing Obamacare 2.0 would screw over the very people to whom they promised to repeal it. For every Nancy Pelosi, there is a Tom Garrett, for every John Lewis there is an Justin Amash, the list goes on and while it is a short list, at least there is a list. These representatives lose seats on committees, they lose donors, but most dangerously the cartel goes after their reputations and that of their families. You play stupid games you get stupid prizes. Politicians who play the games get perks but the people get nothing more than some pork barrel spending to tidy them over until the next election. The cartel rewards loyalty despite the American people getting shafted twenty ways to Sunday. President Trump calls D.C. "The Swamp" and honestly I find that to be offensive to actual swamps because an alligator has never extorted money from me, calling it an income tax, nor have any other swamp creatures tried to infringe on my individual liberty.

Many Republicans and Democrats attempt to make the argument that their battle is an ideological one with a line drawn in the sand, but while they give their base the mental catnip needed to drive up their war-chest and coffers for the next election, they are instead finding ways to exploit the system. This is the history of partisans in the political arena, just look at the dictators and cabals in charge of any nation under the rule of communism and see how they lived, ate, and enjoyed life while others suffered.

Animal Farm by George Orwell is the most perfect example of the utopianism that progressives and conservatives tout. "All animals are equal but some are more equal than others" says the pigs, who declare themselves the self-appointed elite in charge of the farm who force the other animals to labor while they sit around, get drunk and sleep in beds (one of the first established rules the pigs made), eventually committing a cardinal sin on Animal Farm- cut deals with the humans who they fought a bloody revolution against to earn their freedom. When Obamacare was passed, the Democrats who pushed it down our throats and said it was that or harsh penalties gave themselves exceptions from the forced mandate. The funny tale of Republican Congressman Tim Murphy showed a legislator at the federal level attempt to push through federal abortion bans, but ended up impregnating a mistress and scolding her to get an abortion.

Rand Paul is right that government is a machine, it can kill and can save, it can create and can destroy, but when you have to worry about whether or not the next person will use it responsibly or use it for ill purpose, you already have more problems than you realize. Most progressives and conservatives get offended when libertarians blame the government for some or every issue that comes about, because everyone has their favorite agency or sacred cow that can do no wrong, because of that they aren't open for fair discourse because they already have a firm opposition to you in their minds.

That is the issue that libertarians have the hardest time communicating to people, they discuss "the state" as if it is a living, breathing entity and when they discuss it people imagine images of monsters in their closet or a literal, Hydra like creature consuming every part of society. It sounds more ridiculous than it really is because regular people don't think the angry lady at the DMV is part of some plot to enslave the population. In reality it is less sophisticated but even more disgusting, because the abuse of power and influence that actually goes on, most people haven't witnessed outside of episodes of *House of Cards*. The government isn't the specific danger, the people in charge of it are what enable the system to become dangerous. Because government is abused and used beyond its boundaries, it's powers meant to protect the people are instead use to coerce them.

The cartel runs your schools, the media, the cops, every part of your daily existence is in some way, shape, or form forced to interact with some aspect of them. This is why our Founding Fathers pleaded with us to stay vigilant, to avoid situations where government could get out of control and break out of its constitutional barriers. The state is a mechanism of force, violence, and coercion, but what makes it dangerous at the end of the day is like a driver to a car, or a madman to a weapon, it is all about the individuals in the seat of power, the seat the Washington Cartel will fight to a bloody pulp to keep.

Governor Buddy Roemer once discussed this topic of the wheeling and dealing that goes on in the swamp, saying "if you think Washington D.C. is a fair shake, if you think Washington D.C. is on the level, you just don't understand what happens in America. It's the few elites at the top, no one else counts. I have decided, I did it about a year ago, the only way to bring change was to stand up." Until man is truly overcome by our better angels, it is better to have a purposeful and watchful eye on those in public positions, and to never fall into the trap of thinking you just need the right person or group of people to find the solutions to all of society's problems.

Where government expands and deepens, individual liberty shrinks, and whether your team wears red or blue, everyone loses something when we play Russian roulette with the state.

85

Chapter 10: It's the Libertarian's Fault

"We are blinded in our history what used to work." ~John McAfee

It was hot and humid, I hadn't shaved either so I looked like a sweaty Mexican day laborer walking up to the door of this random house in this well to do Northern Virginia neighborhood. It was the first campaign I actually worked on, and knocking on doors in the blistering heat was not what the job description listed when I applied to be a policy analyst. Campaigns are weird like that, one minute you apply to just make phone calls and next you realize now you're in charge of a whole bunch of random people and you're running between two different offices, going on radio to stump for your boss, and running another twenty odd jobs a day that are thrown at you. If you ever run into a person working on a campaign, buy them coffee, those folks are working a very thankless job-assuming they get paid.

In 2015, my brother stayed involved with the Libertarian Party after the 2014 Sarvis senate campaign and recruited me after my internship at FreedomWorks ended. Brian Suojanen, tech entrepreneur during the week and motorcycle enthusiast by weekend was running for House of Delegates in an off year election. This meant two things, no one was interested in politics, and they didn't want to even think about politics either. Virginia is cursed, we have elections all the freaking time, its like a never ending cycle.

I walked for hours in the blistering heat with Brian and Ryan and wasn't getting much of a friendly vibe except for one woman who kindly offered to fill up my tumbler bottle with some ice. In 2015, the national opioid epidemic was starting to become noticeable, but still wasn't an issue that got people's blood boiling compared to other issues like what bathroom men pretending to be women can use, or whether to build a wall along Canada or Mexico first.

After spending several years next to Selma, it became abundantly clear to me that the war on drugs was a complete failure. Apart from the racial bias in arrests, the harsh mandatory minimum sentencing that would give a life sentence to a 17 year old for holding a little bit of pot while slapping a few years on a rapist, not to mention the massive waste of our tax dollars to go after harmless people growing a plant and then throwing them into the slammer with hard core gangbangers, I never understood why we had to punish people who are obviously inflicting more harm on themselves than others. Anyone that has ever walked through a jail or rehab facility will tell you this isn't a criminal justice issue, this is a public health issue. The only party in America it seemed willing to confront this issue head on was the Libertarian Party, and for that I felt it was my duty to discuss an issue that didn't directly affect my life, but an issue I saw affect millions of Americans.

The last door I knocked on that day was the most memorable, the owner of the house opened the door and the first thing I saw was a giant pot leaf image on his shirt. This was gold, this would be the house where I earned Brian a supporter.

"Hello sir! I'm Remso with the Brian Suojanen campaign..." he cut me off.

"What party is he?" he asked with a grin, I smiled thinking this was my way in.

"Libertarian" I replied proudly.

"Nope, sorry" he said while attempting to slam the door. Now I did something you should never, ever do; I grabbed the door before he could close it.

"But you have a pot leaf on your shirt!" I pleaded, thinking this potential senior stoner would take sympathy on my sweaty face.

"Libertarians never win, you just split the votes so Republicans can win," he said and then finally managed to close the door. That was rich, I'd heard for years Libertarians are Democrats that like guns, now I was being told we were essentially Republicans who liked pot. We get blamed literally for everything it seems, there was even an original graphic novel published a while back which accused the 2008 financial crash and bank bailouts on the existence of the book "Atlas Shrugged". If someone doesn't like you already, they'll always find something to pin you on no matter how stupid.

One thing about life before the 2016 election was that not only did most of America not know what libertarians were or what that word even meant, they probably had never met an actual libertarian either. If they did, they were probably buying *InfoWars* water filters and discussing FEMA concentration camps. The media and the two establishment parties have always told people what libertarians were without ever meeting, speaking to, or getting to know an actual libertarian. Libertarians were like Bigfoot or Chupacabra, heard of but never seen except for maybe the shadowy corners of Ron Paul rallies, perhaps a deep south militia, or buying drugs on the dark web.

In 2014 at MMI, I actually dressed as a libertarian for Halloween. I wore an American flag bandana, a Sarvis 2013 t-shirt Ryan had sent me, and my ACU patterned pants with a cardboard sign that said "End the Fed!" to boot. I'm pretty sure I walked around with a stereo playing an episode of *InfoWars*. The guys in my barracks laughed, I laughed, it was funny. Sadly, that is the image that comes up in most people's minds when the word "libertarian" is uttered. It's never Milton Friedman or F.A. Hayek, it's always Alex Jones or the naked guy from the 2016 Libertarian National Convention who stripped on live TV.

In 2013, my family drove down with my soon to be roommate's family (a match made in Hell). I don't remember how we became roommates, but his dad met my dad and they thought we'd be good roommates. Advice to the wise from the stupid, never let your parents pick your roommate. This guy, let's call him "Jack", was in a different platoon during basic at Ft. Knox that summer with me, so I thought it kinda made sense. I rode with him and his dad to get to know them a bit better as we drove from North Carolina to Alabama. Here you had a very wealthy, conservative, evangelical family, and then my family, who didn't think gay people broke into your house to suck your blood and redo your closet at night. Maybe I thought I shouldn't believe in stereotypes because that would be rude, but maybe if I had I would have been more prepared for what happened next.

"Would you ever date a black girl?" Jack's dad said, sitting in the front passenger seat, turning his head to look at me as if I were being interrogated. In my mind I was thinking where in the world did that question come from? Five minutes ago he said I had bad taste in music because I liked the Black Keys. I was kinda taken aback. he said it in a tone that one would use to ask if their kids were smoking pot or if Sam got a little too close to Pam on prom night.

"Yes, if she was a good girl and we liked each other I would date her regardless of race," I replied. I could see Jack's face in the reflection on the windshield turn to shock and his dad continued to look at me as if I had just taken a shit in the backseat of the car.

"I think that certain people should stay with those of their own kind since it would be disrespectful to one's family to mix outside their race," he said with a straight face. This wasn't that long ago, this was 2013 and this guy was looking at me as if I was one bad answer away from getting lynched. It was also incredibly disrespectful since he knew my father was half latino and my mother was half asian. I'm not exactly the whitest piece of wood on the white picket fence as I was constantly reminded by other kids growing up.

Side note, later in the year I went on a date with a beautiful girl who happened to be black while I lived in Alabama. She was a classy young woman and fun to be around, and while we never went on a date after that, I do remember her asking what my parents thought about dating someone outside your race. "It's not something that ever occurred to me growing up being an issue," I said. As a young bachelor I went on dates with different types of women, I even went on one date with a girl at Liberty University who was Puerto Rican and she said, "I want to be with someone more Spanish" (I know, kinda rude). People naturally want to put everyone in boxes based on everything from politics to race to what baseball team you like. Imagine if we just treated people like people, but maybe that's just too utopian to pull off.

The questions continued from my view of drugs, prostitution, and war. According to Jack later that day I gave all the "wrong answers." Well if my answers were wrong, I didn't want to be right, and if Jack's way was the way of the Lord, I think he may have missed some sermons because people stopped calling him by his name and started calling him "Mr. Sexual Assault" until he flunked out of school. You learn a lot about yourself in college, and I learned I never wanted to be near that piece of shit again for as long as I lived. Going back to Jack's dad, he even had issues with Rand Paul on every issue under the sun, thinking that Rand Paul would intentionally go against every Republican bill in the senate because he was secretly an anarchist, or a Democrat infiltrator. I bring this up because the immoral, depraved and crazy libertarian stereotype is real in the minds of many Americans.

Yes, I don't believe in the war on drugs because it is an institutionalized failure and harms more people than it is intended to save. Yes, we need to the rethink the laws pertaining to what consenting adults do in the bedroom, because two adults should not be imprisoned for consensual acts and maybe if you pull it out from under the shadows, you'll have less murders, pimps, diseases, and human trafficking. Just because I think it is morally disgusting doesn't mean I believe it is worth sticking someone in prison for. Yes, I believe that we should only go to war with congressional approval when we have been aggressed upon, not just bomb indiscriminately because we don't like how someone talks. In conversation, most people would stop listening after I said the prostitution part. You know who else believes that? Ron Paul, a man who is a devout Christian and has been faithful in his marriage to his wife for almost half a century, but please, go around telling everyone how I want prostitutes on every street corner.

I always thought it was hypocritical that so many pro-life Republicans can be so pro-war and ignore the lives of all the brown kids in the Middle East we injure and leave orphaned as "collateral damage", but maybe that's just me. I've never done drugs, never had sex with a prostitute, nor wanted to stay out of war because I somehow didn't support the troops. Libertarians support individual liberty not because we support every free decision you can make, but because we believe that you should live your life without government restriction as long as you respect the liberty of others and not hurt people or take their stuff.

Congressman Tom Garrett of Virginia, one of the most pro-liberty leaders in the House of Representatives, member of the House Freedom Caucus, and a self-identified "conservatarian"[17] (i.e. conservative with strong libertarian leanings) understands this backlash more than most. In Garrett's first term he opposed Trumpcare (which many Republicans weren't happy with) which meant somehow he was anti-Trump. Then he fought and led the effort for federal decriminalization of marijuana (which many Republicans weren't happy with) which meant somehow he was now pro-pot. He even supported a bill which explicitly said to stop arming terrorists and potential terrorists with weapons for crying out loud, and Republicans really didn't know what mental gymnastics to pull over that when the McCains of the world got their panties in a wad. Garrett has been chastised by his own party for his civil libertarian beliefs, and those like him like Paul, Amash, and Massie are always the first one's to blame when the GOP doesn't get their way on some big government policy.

I've been in situations where one person will accuse me of being a bleeding heart liberal and another person will call me ultra-conservative. Because everyone is so stuck within the left-right spectrum, it doesn't only confuse them when they meet a

---

[17] Conservatanan was thrown around during the 2012 Ron Paul campaign to describe his supporters, and was later made popular by National Review editor Charles C.W. Cooke in his book the Conservatarian Manifesto, 2015.

libertarian, but it frustrates the Hell out of them because somehow, they literally can't comprehend how someone can opt out of the false, fixed worldview where you only have one of two political sides to pick from and accept their ideas wholesale. You can customize your clothes down to the zipper color, have a million ways to order your coffee from Starbucks, customize a car, but you have to stick to only one of two political beliefs? Who actually buys into conservative or liberal beliefs 100%? It's like when the Republican Party called pornography a public health crisis at their convention in 2016. I dare anyone to sample the web history of half the male delegates who voted on that and tell me what pops up. When it comes to the third largest voting block in America, Independents, the two parties even feel that they own your votes.

Case in point, it was Election Day in 2015 for the Virginia midterms[18], and the results of the 87th legislative district were 8,203 votes for Democrat John Bell, 7,883 votes for Republican Chung Nguyen, and 343 votes for good old Libertarian Brian.

"Wow!" Brian said over the phone. "That was 342 more than I expected."

The crap that began to fly from Republicans was fast and furious, they put in more effort into complaining than they did campaigning. I saw in a newspaper or article somewhere written by a Republican operative that "if the Libertarian hadn't ran in the race, they [voters] would have voted Republican." Each time I see or hear someone say that I imagine Wolverine slowly running his adamantium claws down a chalkboard sadistically creating that wretched noise. I remember meeting voters, talking to locals, and I can promise you that if they had not voted Libertarian, they certainly would not have voted Republican because the problem is they most likely would not have voted at all. "It's the Libertarians' fault the Republican lost," is what I hear constantly, as if grown adults are incapable of deciding who they want to vote for.

In 2013, this was the same case to a larger degree. Democrat Terry McAuliffe got 47.8% of the vote, Ken Cuccinelli got 45.2%, and Robert Sarvis received 6.5%. Sarvis[19] received more votes for statewide office than any Libertarian in US history at that time. As soon as the results were in, the screaming started too across every right wing outlet on the east coast. "Sarvis stole Republican votes!" one radio host yelled for hours on end. Let's take it down a notch, you can't steal Republican votes because Republicans don't own votes as much as Democrats own votes (though sometimes Democrats literally steal votes, go look at Kennedy in 1960 during that election for a fun story). More registered Democrats voted for Sarvis than registered Republicans, and independent voters made up most of his support. If Republicans in Sarvis' 2013 race and Brian's 2015 race had taken time to actually talk to the voters that voted Libertarian, they would have figured out why pretty easily. In 2018, progressive economist Robert Reich did a video[20]

[18] https://www.vpap.org/candidates/261405/elections/

[19] https://ballotpedia.org/Robert_Sarvis

[20] https://www.occupy.com/article/robert-reich-should-you-vote-third-party-video#sthash.7HA1zNZJ.dpbs

where he blamed the third party candidacy of Ralph Nader in 2000 for siphoning votes from Al Gore, and Gary Johnson and Jill Stein in 2016 for siphoning votes from Hillary Clinton. Even supposedly smart people can fall into the lies propped up by party elites who feel entitled to your votes.

From 2012 onward, disappointment and disenfranchisement among the two major parties reached higher levels each election. In 2013, LGBTQ rights were still a hot button topic only Sarvis covered. Sarvis was also the only candidate to take a stance on Virginia's looming state pension crisis. While the other candidates were trying to demonize each other, Sarvis took on the tough issues head on. Brian Suojanen was the only candidate to take a firm stance on not only the war on drugs, but also on Eminent Domain and Civil Asset Forfeiture, two very hot button issues neither his opponents took a stance on until a few weeks before the election. When Sarvis ran for US Senate in 2014, he was the only candidate in the race to call out President Barack Obama's intervention against ISIL, calling for a congressional approval for military action in Syria as per the Constitution while Republican Ed Gillespie and Democrat John Warner stayed silent on the matter.

The establishment parties didn't allow Sarvis into any of the major debates in either 2013 or 2014, except for some low key public forums most people didn't know about where candidates weren't even allowed to debate or address each other. This is the biggest scam that goes back to another lie, the lie that Libertarians can't win. Libertarians aren't allowed to win in the minds of the establishment parties which is why the goal post to participate changes each time a Libertarian gets involved in an election. One minute a Libertarian is a "non-factor" as 2013 Republican candidate for governor, Ken Cuccinelli, labeled Sarvis in June of that year, but then after the election, a Virginia Republican Committee member went to *Newsmax* and blamed Sarvis and Libertarian voters for Cuccinelli's loss to McAuliffe.

The Republican monopoly on conservative votes alone is always in question unlike the Democratic Party. Republicans just can't seem to ever keep it together when another more conservative or liberty minded candidate jumps on the table. William F. Buckley didn't even run for office as a Republican when he campaigned for Mayor of New York City; Buckley ran as the nominee for the Conservative Party of New York because the Republican running was more progressive than the Democrat. Was Buckley "stealing" Republican votes or did the Republicans not put up a real conservative candidate for other Republicans to get behind?

To an extent, the "Libertarians can't win" argument is true because the feats they have to jump to get on the ballot are remarkably tougher than Republicans and Democrats, and then if they are seen as a threat, they aren't allowed to participate in public debates with them most the time either. In 2014, both the Warner and Gillespie senate campaigns told the hosts of a debate at Virginia Tech behind closed doors that they wouldn't participate if Sarvis was allowed on stage. How can you win an election when the opposing parties make it difficult to compete, and then work together to prevent you from standing on an equal public forum? The Commission on Presidential Debates (CPD) alone is black eye on our Republic often ignored.

Founded after the 1992 election, the Republicans and Democrats met in the dark to create an organization that would become the de facto head of all public presidential debates in the future in order to prevent third party and independent candidates from ever threatening establishment control again after dealing with the popular independent candidate and founder of the Reform Party, Ross Perot. Perot received 19% of the popular vote against George H.W. Bush and Bill Clinton. Perot drew on support from working class voters who were disappointed with Bush's involvement in NAFTA and those that worried Clinton's dubious and suspicious past as Governor of Arkansas would leak into the White House. Because neither Bush or Clinton received more than half the popular vote (despite Clinton's ultimate Electoral College success) the Democrats' and Republicans' mutual love of larger government created this arcane institution to prevent another Ross Perot from threatening the duopoly's monopoly of power.

The CPD determines every factor that goes into qualifications for debate access, even down to choosing which polls to use (which then never announce in advance) in order to assess who has reached the 15% public interest margin just to obtain entrance. In terms of the polls, numerous media outlets don't even include third party candidates. Gary Johnson was left out of most the polls conducted by the mainstream media outlets in 2016, which meant most voters weren't given an option beyond Trump or Clinton unless you count "undecided."

Republicans don't lose elections because Libertarians steal votes, they lose because they didn't get enough votes, they lose like everyone else loses, some people just can't grasp that first grade understanding of losing. Conservative author Ann Coulter is one of those individuals that need to go back to first grade. During the 2014 race, Coulter wrote[21] on her website "if you are considering voting for the Libertarian candidate in any Senate election, please send me your name and address so I can track you down and drown you." *Reason* contributor Ronald Bailey obliged, publishing his name and Virginia home address stating publicly that he would be voting for Robert Sarvis, and that he would "see you [Coulter] soon." There was a joke in my house that year that if you went into the bathroom and turned the lights off and said "Ann Coulter" three times, she would pop out of the mirror and drown you in the toilet. This type of crap was funny but not funny at the same time, but we went with it.

Libertarians and third party candidates in general aren't simply a protest vote, but are a serious option for voters that go unnoticed on issues the other parties aren't willing to discuss, thus bringing out people that otherwise would not have voted at all. The Democrat that beat Brian came over to him at a function before the election and said that if Brian's campaign hadn't put out videos online, he wouldn't have produced a single

---

[21] http://reason.com/blog/2014/09/18/anne-coulter-wants-to-drown-libertarians

campaign commercial during his entire run. Libertarians keep the process competitive and the two major parties accountable. The Democrat victor even mentioned that Brian was the reason he changed his mind on civil asset forfeiture reform, voting for multiple reform measures to reign it in during his first term in the House of Delegates instead of voting to maintain it was we warned voters he would have.

Why would anyone put themselves in the crosshairs of Republicans and Democrats knowing the game is rigged against them? Sarvis wrote a series of op-eds at the *Collegiate Times* in 2015, part one was titled *the Trials and Tribulations of Third-Party Politics*[22]. At the beginning of his political career, Sarvis was a Republican, and for the most part viewed politics like most Americans did, stating "I was as disdainful of third parties as most people are. When I first ran for office in 2011 [ran for Virginia State Senate as a Republican] I didn't even consider running outside the major two parties." So what caused the conversion? For Sarvis it was obvious, "as a candidate, I saw up close and personally, the Republican and Democratic parties of Virginia. I was totally turned off by the hypocrisy, the extremism, ignorance and corruption in both parties."

2016 was the first election in several decades where third party candidates were a major force among voters. Many right wing contributors went to war with each other regarding the #NeverTrump movement, where pro-trump commentators drew a line in the sand and said that a vote for Gary Johnson (Libertarian), Darrell Castle (Constitution Party), Evan McMullin (Independent), or Jill Stein (Green Party) was a vote for Hillary Clinton. That logic, taken as is, would imply if I chose not to eat from McDonalds, and instead chose to eat at Taco Bell, somehow Burger King made money. I voted for Evan McMullin in 2016 because I did not feel the Libertarian nominee Gary Johnson and his pro-Clinton running mate Bill Weld, positively promoted a libertarian agenda to the masses, instead promoting some form of low tax progressivism. I didn't vote for Donald Trump because I felt he was a weak candidate who didn't have a grasp on the issues. I didn't vote for Hillary Clinton because she was a criminal who had evaded the justice system for decades. I voted for McMullin because I thought he was bright and his values and message matched mine. My vote for McMullin didn't help Trump and it didn't help Hillary. My vote may "not have mattered" as some will say, but it was my vote and it mattered to me. Your vote is your vote, candidates have to earn it, not just expect it when the election comes around.

What was hilarious was that Clinton supporters loved the idea of third party candidates getting in the race because it would drain "Trump votes." The day after the 2016 election when the Johnson-Weld ticket gained 3% of the popular vote, Clinton supporters foamed at the mouth and screamed to the heavens saying that Gary Johnson was the reason Hillary lost because he took "Hillary's votes." I've worked in Independent, Libertarian, and Republican campaigns (I even once endorsed a Green Party candidate running for state office in Arizona) and never once did I meet someone that

---

[22] http://www.collegiatetimes.com/opinion/robert-sarvis-part-i-the-trials-and-tribulations-of-third/article_966443d4-d405-11e4-80d1-f3bd890d1ebd.html

voted a certain way because they wanted to swing an election for someone else to support the person they actually liked because no one is that freaking stupid.

I'd be lying if I said the stupid "vote stealing" argument was exclusive to Republicans and Democrats even though they are the biggest culprits. During the GOP primaries, I received many vicious and vile messages regarding my vote for Ted Cruz on Primary Day in Virginia because I was "casting a vote meant for Rand Paul" because "this is Rand's time!" Let's remember at that point, Rand Paul dropped out of the race immediately after the Iowa Caucus (which Cruz won handedly) several months back. There is such a thing as a vote that doesn't matter though: it's voting for someone who isn't even running anymore, but some Rand Paul supporters didn't care and voted for Rand after he dropped out because they wanted to flip the bird to everyone. There is a saying in politics, don't treat your 80% friend like a 20% enemy. Some people will never get past the 20% differences they have, but those people don't matter that much anyway because they don't see the bigger picture. A truly hilarious moment came a few weeks before the 2016 election when polling in Utah (a state where Republicans were concerned McMullin would win) showed Evan McMullin outpolling Gary Johnson. I saw too many people I once deemed as intelligent individuals go full moron and scream, "He's stealing Gary Johnson's votes!"

A true blue American and friend of mine, Scott Rupert, was a staunch constitutionalist that ran for US Senate in Ohio in 2016 as an Independent. Scott said something which has stuck with me over the years. In a campaign commercial, Scott stated:

> For years the Republican and Democratic parties have used social issues and crisis to keep us at odds with one another. They've divided us in groups and pit each group against the other while those in government have together collaborated to strip us of our liberty little by little... Government of, by, and for the people requires our participation, not as voters but as leaders and decision makers. But the parties have made it difficult for ordinary Americans to do so...The message is simple, the Constitution protects every American equally, but its powerless to protect itself, that's our job, and it's time we take it seriously.

Blaming libertarians for anything is actually a way for me to justify calling you a moron. There aren't enough libertarians in the country to make any severe or immediate changes, and even then its not this morally relative, postmodern agenda they are accused of promoting. I can assure you there aren't libertarians selling hookers, drugs, and guns in exchange for Bitcoin to teenagers next to the school playground. Sarvis, in the third part of his op-ed series, touched on this issue nicer than I have, saying "I don't begrudge anyone on their bad judgements, but the tunnel-visioned, win-at-all-costs mentality of the two-party system drove many of them, both activists and members of the conservative media, to slander my campaign by explicitly lying about my policy positions. It is shady business, this politics." It amazes me time and time again how people who are your allies and friends one minute turn to hate you the next minute once you step out of the two-party gladiator pit.

Libertarian Party candidates are elected once every blue moon and often to local offices people didn't think existed. Unlike Republicans and Democrats, Libertarians haven't had the chance to bankrupt the country, steal our liberties, or cause the deaths of thousands of innocent people. Republicans and Democrats are doing a great job at screwing up our country leaving little room for third parties to contribute the the orchestra of chaos and betrayal.

Blame the libertarians all you want for whatever you want, because saying a lie long enough still doesn't make it true at all. Sarvis said it best, "Recognize that your vote is never thrown away if you're voting for the candidate you think is best."

In a *Washington Post*[23] op-ed supporting Sarvis for governor in 2013, famous conservative commentator George Will (who would several years later become a self-identified libertarian) said "Sarvis is enabling voters to register dissatisfaction with the political duopoly. Markets are information-generating mechanisms, and Virginia's political is sending, through Sarvis, signals to the two durable parties."

[23] https://www.washingtonpost.com/opinions/george-f-will-robert-sarvis-virginias-other-choice-for-governor/2013/10/23/1544f8d6-3b5c-11e3-b6a9-da62c264l40e_story.html?noredirect=on&utm_term=.50f915e8e1d9

Chapter 11: Internet Killed the Video Star

"Telling the truth is fun" ~Andrew Brietbart

Libertarian content in the mainstream media and online in the mid 2000's was a lot like alternative cigarettes: they were difficult to find, probably falsely advertised, and left a really bad taste in your mouth. You knew what the real thing was, you wanted it, but you couldn't find it and if you did, it was crappy, sketchy, and a complete turn off.

Libertarians, as I've mentioned repeatedly, have never had a fair shake at telling their story. After the 2012 election, the dawn of the internet opened up new opportunities to allow everyday people a chance to go out and reach the eyes and ears of millions. John Stossel on *Fox Business* was for many years the only openly libertarian program on TV. His show was groundbreaking because it wasn't about attacking Republicans or attacking Democrats, instead Stossel went straight to the source- out of control government trying to dictate the lives of everyday Americans and even those across our borders. Compared to screaming and ranting Alex Jones, Stossel was a calm, breath of fresh air, pointing to proven facts instead of conspiracies, doing actual journalism instead of just commentary, and making the program content accessible to everyone. Stossel's success was a rising tide that rose all boats and led to Greg Gutfeld's show *Redeye, The Independents*, and *Kennedy w/ Lisa Kennedy*.

The success of Stossel showed there was a thirst for libertarian content, and with that, a grassroots movement led by activist Austin Petersen helped push an obscure libertarian judge from the silence of the internet into the limelight on the most hardcore libertarian show in television history- *Freedom Watch w/ Judge Andrew Napolitano*.

Like all things however, mainstream television has a shelf life. *Redeye* was cancelled, *The Independents* was cancelled, the Judge's show was canned, and eventually Stossel left Fox, leaving Kennedy to be the last libertarian on that network.

I mention this not as a history lesson, but as a point. Libertarians cannot expect the mainstream media to give them what they want, much less provide it in a fair and respectable way. The dawn of the internet has shown that the market, left untampered, will always provide. Petersen, who was the Judge's producer, would go on to start *The Libertarian Republic* and his own podcast *Freedom Report* which is one of the most downloaded libertarian podcasts online. Stossel went on and started to do online videos for *Reason TV*.

Reason Magazine was started in 1968 in order to provide a libertarian alternative to many of the more right wing publications such as *National Review*. There was the *Freeman* published by the Foundation for Economic Education, but *Reason* always stuck out for its willingness to cover more taboo issues such as culture and the drug war. Reading *Reason* was how I learned about the Cato Institute, and the rest is history. *The American Conservative*, founded in 2003 as a publication to provide a conservative voice against the Iraq war, while not an explicitly libertarian outlet, has always been fair to libertarian commentators and contributors, often providing a breath of fresh air in terms of political discourse, lending itself to libertarians as a platform often to comment on the war state and other issues of economics and such. These outlets, while the standard of excellence, were once the only places libertarians could find refuge.

Around the same time Petersen launched *The Libertarian Republic*, *Being Libertarian* (originally a satire page to counteract popular Facebook pages such as Being Liberal) grew out of a hobby and into an internationally respected libertarian publication, even launching a very popular multimedia network that has reached millions of viewers. The internet did for libertarians what killing the FCC Fairness Doctrine under the Reagan administration did for talk radio, it unleashed a flood of content and voices upon the world that has changed the game permanently. Podcasting, once a very misunderstood form of broadcasting, now enabled anybody to pick up a microphone and reach an audience. These days, one in five Americans listens to a podcast series regularly.

Hollywood began to take notice (to an extent) and the interest in dystopian films in the vein of *1984* began to pop up such as *the Giver, Hunger Games, Divergent*, along with a string of other franchises that always showed a fascist government dictating and controlling the lives of the people, and a growing resistance that would rise up and fight back. Strangely, many of these films are held in special regard by progressives, who still fail to see the road to serfdom and the techniques used to control the masses. Progress is progress however, and even if Hollywood is making these films simply to make a buck, the demand shows that the people want more.

When I came back to Alabama after Cato University that summer, to say I was saddened having been deprived of like minded company would be an understatement. I went on my phone's podcast app and put in the search bar "libertarian" and the first show that popped up was an interview with historian Dr. Tom Woods on a show called *Lions of Liberty*. From that first episode I was hooked. Who or what was *Lions of Liberty*? A Koch brothers project? A beltway think tank? Neck bearded anarchists living in their basement? Literally none of that, just some average Joes who love liberty.

Lions wasn't the first libertarian podcast out there, but it sits upon a pedestal of prominence in the world of libertarian content. Marc Clair, Howie Snowden, John Odermatt, and Brian McWilliams met when they were students at Penn State, and years later they encountered the Ron Paul campaign. Swept up with the rush of fun and excitement the ideas of Dr. Paul's campaign promoted, they started a website called *Lions of Liberty* (the lion inspired by Penn State's mascot the Nittany Lion) so they could continue to promote these ideas. The website over time developed into the flagship *Lions of Liberty* podcast hosted by Marc Clair. Through Marc Clair's one-on-one interviews, libertarians across the country and around the world have been introduced to the many movers and shakers in the Liberty movement who have a direct effect on the world around us. Many have tried to copy Marc's formula, but very few have succeeded.

Several years into the main show, they launched its first spinoff *Felony Fridays* hosted by John Odermatt.

John, neither a cop, lawyer, or anyone that has spent a day in the justice system, was pulled into the broken criminal justice system when his brother-in-law was tricked by a undercover vice cop into essentially becoming the middle man between the cop and a local drug dealer. Seeing how the criminal justice system used and abused him and the toll it cost on his family, John now uses Felony Friday's as an outlet to allow those in a position of change to tell their stories and hopefully help someone down the road.

Brian McWilliam's was the most recent spinoff with his show *Electric Liberty Land*, a current events and comedy show filling the sea of dark, dreary, and often far-too-academic libertarian podcasts with something to laugh along, learn, and enjoy

When I started the *Remso Republic* in 2016, there were probably a few dozen active libertarian podcasts online. I started my show because I saw how the mainstream media and political elite treat underdog candidates and bright people with unconventional ideas, I wanted to give them a voice. These days, there is a new libertarian podcast or YouTube show out every week, the list now is probably longer than anyone ever anticipated. It's a good time for liberty, because the more freedom oriented content, the better.

The media and entertainment realm has often been ignored by conservatives and libertarians alike and hasn't been truly embraced until recently. With social media censorship and corporate control of the television industry, it is becoming increasingly difficult to spread these pro-freedom ideas online. What used to represent free expression and democratization of information now represents social manipulation and deceptive intentions by the very people in charge of these platforms such as Mike Zuckerberg, who beg of you to trust them.

Where once Facebook was the only multi-feature social media platform on the web, we now have platforms such as Minds. Founded by Minds CEO Bill Ottman, John Ottman, and Mark Harding in 2012, Minds launched publicly in 2015. In 2017, Minds was the fastest project to raise over a million dollars in funding in Equity Crowdfunding. While Bill Ottman and Minds is not explicitly libertarian, their purpose and Minds' function is. According to Ottman during the beginning phases of Minds, "traditional social media networks are overrun with surveillance, censorship, demonetization and restrictive algorithms. Minds solves these problems with free and open source software, free speech policy, anonymity, encryption and decentralization."

When Twitter began massive censorship on their platform along with removing the verification badges for various pages, a new Twitter alternative called Gab, proclaiming to be the free speech platform popped up. What's funny is that the mainstream media tried to label Gab a white supremacist, alt-right platform because of some of the initial users that jumped on after being banned on Twitter, but what I've seen having my own Gab account is that when you compare it to any other social media platform, you will always find the same amount of terrible and disgusting people everywhere. Every social media platform is filled with some degree of filth, but because of the institutionalization of Facebook and Twitter, somehow they aren't responsible for what people do or say on their platforms but everyone else is, this is done because the corporations and the elites want you to stay on their internet plantation. I still have a Facebook and Twitter account, but my content is often hampered in reach thanks to algorithms or pinched because of censorship, don't even get me started about verification. Minds and Gab promise one thing and one thing only, you control your content and no one will tell you what you can't say. That promise alone is enough to get me onboard.

One situation sparked outrage in the libertarian community in 2017, when Austin Petersen (now running for US Senate as a Republican) was removed from Facebook for thirty days for supposedly breaking Facebook's rules and user conditions for posting a picture of a AR-15. It was later reported by *Fox News*[24] that Facebook's Chief Operating Officer, Sheryl Sandberg, had donated $5,400 to Petersen's Democrat opponent Claire McCaskill.

Collusion much?

Petersen (far from the definition of an alt-right type of guy) stated that Facebook's censorship pushed him to establish a foothold on Gab in order to maintain a social media presence. No wonder the mainstream media and the powerful social media platforms hate the up and comers, they are a direct threat to not only their bottom line, but their ability to control and watch us.

Libertarians are now entering the age where they no longer have to ask permission to build a platform and cultivate an audience around their ideas, and for this reason, the genie has left the bottle and now libertarians and even conservatives have full control to dictate their own paths and tell their own stories.

---

[24] http://www.foxnews.com/politics/2017/09/28/republican-senate-candidate-in-missouri-says-facebook-banned-him-over-ar-15-giveaway.html

Chapter 12: Macho Flash

"Because brutalism is the outlying impulse in the libertarian world- young people are no longer in with this whole approach. It behaves the way we've come to expect from seriously marginalized groups." ~Jeffrey Tucker

I love the film *Mean Girls* and if you understand that movie, you understand how cults, frats, and political parties manage to get around in civilized society. Regular middle class people accept and ignore bad behavior, sometimes justifying it because they don't want to become a victim or feel they can get something out of it. There is a part in the film where one girl discusses one of the mean, popular girls at school, Regina George, and says "one time, she punched me in the face. It was awesome." In 2016, I stopped pretending I liked the Libertarian Party (LP) punching my hopes and dreams in the face, and I left that mess behind faster than a bat out of Hell. I can report that several years later, I haven't regretted the decision to livestream myself shredding my Libertarian Party membership card once. The Libertarian Party was my Regina George, only less attractive and not rich or influential.

One of the characters from *Mean Girls* discusses the problems with Regina, saying "Regina George is not sweet! She's a scum-sucking road whore! She ruined my life!" Another girl states the same sentiment less poetically, "She's a life ruiner. She ruins people's lives." Replace "she" and "Regina George" with "Libertarian Party" and I've probably said those exact same things on more than one occasion. There is a reason there are "small l" libertarians and "big L" Libertarians, it is because the libertarians want nothing to do with the Libertarians. The schism in the Liberty movement between Libertarians and libertarians who want to get far away from Libertarians is almost as complicated as libertarianism is made to sound.

Since the Libertarian Party's birth, libertarians have wondered whether or not forming a political party around one, singular ideology would actually turn out to turn into something good. Because of this fight for the identity of the Libertarian Party, it is why so many offshoot libertarian organizations exist outside of partisan politics and more in the realm of journalism and academia. It is why the Koch brother faction hates the Murray Rothbard faction, why the Cato Institute hates the Ludwig Von Mises Institute, and why you have Libertarians and libertarians who are Republicans, or Democrats (I've never met one), or Independents. Even before the Libertarian Party was founded in 1971 there were problems, Von Mises himself called Milton Friedman and the Chicago boys a bunch of socialists. Everyone wants to do things their own way, which brings a unique set of pros and cons in the process.

When you think about it, Republicans have it kind of easy. For example, the Republican Party is made up of a coalition including social traditionalists (social conservatives), free market libertarians (your Friedman types), and anti-communists (neoconservatives). Together they form the Republican Party, and because of their shared majority beliefs regardless of combination, they can all claim to be conservatives. They bicker and fight and gnash at each other's throats from time to time but they are all united in their unquestionable hatred of progressivism and Democrats. Libertarians are a little different, in truth, they don't really like anybody, not even each other, so it is much harder to focus their hatred on any one specific thing. Sadly, it is easier to unite people on what they hate then it is to unite people on what they believe in. I met more Trump supporters in 2016 who voted for him because they hated Hillary than Trump supporters who actually liked him. Mankind is weird, it's because of that weirdness the Libertarian Party exists to kill the dreams of other libertarians from time to time.

The modern Libertarian Party has its own coalition of unique characters- classical liberals, anarcho-capitalists, minarchists, and sadly some socialists who scream nonsense like "I'm anti-capitalist but pro-free market" and "rent is theft!" They can rarely agree on anything because there is a libertarian purity pissing contest going on each time the party gets together to try and do anything. Former 2016 Libertarian presidential candidate John McAfee's VP pick Judd Weiss in 2017 referred to the Libertarian Party[25] as a "chew toy" for Libertarians, and that's the best description I think I've ever heard. LP co-founder and prominent economist and social critic Murray Rothbard once spoke about the types of individuals who because of societal outcasting or other life factors, love and relish being outsiders. Even if they found someone exactly like them, they would do anything and everything possible to force that person away because they can't handle not feeling unique or special. The Libertarian Party from what I encountered is the biggest collection of these people I have ever encountered in my life.

I might as well put up the disclaimer now; Yes, I am an active member of the Republican Party and believe that the GOP is the best way to direct policy in a libertarian direction. There are more libertarians doing good in the GOP than most like to admit. With that said, even though I don't like nor believe in the future success of the Libertarian Party much at all, there are Libertarians who I believe embody the best of libertarian principles and what I value in a statesman, some whom I have and still actively supported in their political endeavors. There was my friend and first campaign boss Brian Suojanen, Robert Sarvis, and even newer faces such as Kevin McCormick in Arizona (who ran for the LP presidential nomination in 2016 and governor of Arizona in 2018), and Larry Sharpe (LP vice presidential candidate and candidate for governor of New York).

Onward, why is the LP unable to get its team together for a united cause unlike the GOP? In 1974, there were some formal and informal agreements in order to prevent the baby political party from fracturing and disappearing into nothingness. In order to create a broader coalition and keep the party together, the larger minarchist bunch and the loud, angry, smaller bunch of anarcho-capitalists agreed to meet in the middle to amend the party platform to become as vague as possible and come up with the more specific

---

[25] http://lionsofliberty.com/2017/04/10/290/

statement of principles that everyone could get behind, thus the Dallas Accord[26] was born. One sentence though is what truly drives the nail in the middle of the whole factionalism within the LP, causing all the hurt feelings and schisms that affect the Liberty movement at large today.

The most controversial statement in the original LP statement of principles that had to be removed thanks to the Dallas Accords was this, "the sole function of government is the protection of…" That sentence alone is the source of most the fighting. Because of an angry, useless group of anarchist ankle biters, the wider majority of minarchists and classical liberals bent over backwards to appease them, and even though they got what they wanted, they haven't even been happy since. In 2016, the anarchist wing of the LP had their own guy gunning for the presidential nomination, and if they had been successful in getting him the LP nomination, the Libertarian Party wouldn't have been able to even petition to get a presidential nominee on the ballot because he refused to file any of the necessary paperwork to be considered a legal candidate because in his anarchist void, no level of federal government should exist, meaning the entire anarchist wing of the Libertarian Party was willing to throw away their chance to make any kind of electoral difference because they'd rather show which among them is more libertarian. The old piece of wisdom that says if you play stupid games you get stupid prizes evades some people far too often.

Within the party there is a term used for this "more libertarian than thou" dick measuring contest called the "Libertarian macho flash" coined by longtime party member Thomas Sipos[27] in 2001 who said "the macho flash is an in-your-face flaunting of the most extreme libertarian hypotheticals." Situations of the macho flash include such occurrences as "should a soccer mom ask about drug policy in a hypothetical libertarian society, the non-flasher will discuss medical marijuana, the failure of Prohibition, and the benefits of treatment over prisons. The macho flasher will defend the right to erect crack cocaine vending machines in daycare centers." Let it sink in, these people don't understand why no one wants to be around them, nonetheless vote for them or donate a penny.

I saw this level of weaponized idiocy in full motion during Brian's campaign in 2015, when Brian was soliciting the homeschool and school choice voters in Virginia who leaned more conservative by pledging to resubmit the Tim Tebow Bill to the general assembly, which would have allowed homeschooled students to participate in public school sports and athletic programs since parents still pay taxes which go towards those schools. The LP secretary for Virginia at the time, who happened to be a well known anarchist and founder of the LP Radical Caucus, went on Brian's official campaign Facebook page, called Brian a fake Libertarian, and then said he couldn't support his campaign because in a libertarian utopia, government schools shouldn't exist and

[26] http://tomwoods.com/d/accord.pdf

[27] http://www.libertarianpeacenik.com/articles/2012/machoflash.html

therefore we should act as if they already don't. This moron went full macho flash and freaked out potential voters, and the horror stories are endless. As someone that has been around the block, I can tell you there is no bigger dumpster fire than the Libertarian Party.

After Brian's campaign I continued blogging since I had a pretty decent social media following. At that point Gary Johnson during a debate with Austin Petersen and John McAfee basically stated he would force Christian bakers to bake gay wedding cakes at the point of a government gun. That statement by Johnson didn't only go against the libertarian view of property rights and voluntary cooperation, but also aggressed upon religious freedom and freedom of conscious. His VP pick, former governor of Massachusetts Bill Weld, was a liberal Republican who wanted a way back into politics. I got tired of the constant bickering and fighting and decided to go independent and support Ted Cruz.

It may sound corny, but I didn't leave the Libertarian Party, the Libertarian Party left me. I was told if I stuck around long enough, I could be a leader within the party and push it towards a new future. I remember I got to address some attendees at the first anniversary of the Libertarian Party headquarters in Alexandria, Virginia, it was so much fun and the air was filled with optimism. According to party leaders I was too much of a statist totalitarian because I said we should promote policies that allowed homeschooled kids to play sports in the public schools their parents pay taxes towards instead of going to every media and newspaper outlet in the Commonwealth and tell everyone we should abolish public education on day one of a Libertarian administration. Brian and his campaign manager were harassed after his campaign by party officials for running a "Republican-lite" campaign. They said we didn't do enough to promote the party, and to that point they were right because we cared more about fighting to represent the interests of the people of the 87th district instead of being simply a fringe political party's brand ambassadors.

One incident I remember back in 2015 was this one LP state senate candidate who was popular for five minutes because his campaign manager filmed a campaign rap video. It was pretty awesome, he seemed like an alright guy. Then everything went to Hell because he accused the Department of Child Protective Services of child abuse and human trafficking, focused his entire campaign on legalizing hard drugs and hookers, and the day before the election, posted a picture of himself having sex with a prostitute. Oh, and he brought a fake eight ball of cocaine to a candidate forum one time. I want to say this dude was ostracized, but no, "he promoted the party and you promoted Republican policies" one state party official told me. Yeah, a family man saying we need to abolish the state income tax is such a Republican ploy. Spare me, please.

A few months after that, an alt-right (at the time no one knew what that word meant) pagan from Florida went into the desert, killed a goat, drank its blood, and did so in order to make some type of deal with the Devil so he could win the Libertarian Party US Senate nomination in Florida (yeah I know Florida has some issues, trust me). Apart from that and some accusations of racism, every news outlet in the country seemed to be talking about the Libertarian who sacrificed a goat so he could fulfill a prophecy of starting WWIII... or was it Civil War II? Things got weird.

Adrian Wyllie, a prominent figure in the LP scene and chairman of the Florida Libertarian Party at the time decided enough was enough and he resigned his position in order to oppose Goat killer dude. Wyllie said in his resignation letter "I once believed this party would always stand unwavering to defend our core principles. Now I know there is little left to defend." Because of a handful of morons, the Libertarian Party and by association the Liberty movement, is tied to this drugged out, anarchist, hooker banging, goat killing stereotype.

But wait! There's more!

It would be a shame if I didn't bring up the naked guy I've been referencing throughout the entire book, James Weeks, the guy that randomly decided to run for the position of Chair of the Libertarian Party, and then next day decided to announce he was dropping out by stripping on national TV and then enlightening us all by saying, "Sorry, that was a dare." One person on Twitter during the incident tweeted, "Is this what it means to #LegalizeFreedom? I have officially seen too much stripping at the Libertarian Convention."

Then the mother of all embarrassing moments happened at *MSNBC* of all places, Gary Johnson's Aleppo moment. *MSNBC* contributor Mike Barnicle asked Johnson "What would you do if you were elected, about Aleppo?" Johnson's face looked like that of a person that literally didn't have a single clue what was going on. Johnson is a very intelligent man, it's sad that most of what is online makes him out to be a joke, but he doesn't help himself sometimes.

"And what is Aleppo?" Johnson asked Barnicle.

"You're kidding" Barnicle snidely replied.

"No," Johnson said; That is where most videos of the "Aleppo moment" as it has been coined, end the clip instead of finishing it off in its entirety. In Johnson's defense, as soon as Barnicle elaborated and stated Aleppo was the epicenter of refugee crisis in Syria, Johnson immediately knew what he was talking about. Most of America had no damn clue what Aleppo was either but suddenly everyone online became a geopolitical expert and knew what Aleppo was. Johnson was laughed at for the rest of the election cycle. The final chapter to that sad campaign came when Bill Weld went on Rachel Maddow's show to gift his underhanded endorsement to Hillary Clinton because he cared more about Trump not becoming president than being a force for libertarian solutions and the Libertarian Party.

Like everything, there are some silver linings, and some Libertarians are doing the very best they can to try and message better. The Libertarian Party of Washington state and Libertarian Party of New York, for the most part, have their act together and are able to not only influence policy, but sometimes even win some offices. The Libertarian Party

104

however, despite the best intentions of some of its members, has probably lost all credibility. It is heartbreaking that just a handful of bad actors can ruin progress for so many good and dedicated people.

Libertarian Party Vice Chairman Arvin Vohra went on a several month long social media tirade in the summer of 2017 where he equated veterans and military members to child killers and mindless sociopaths[28]. I guess he didn't need them after 2016 when he actively tried to solicit active duty military votes after it was discovered most US service members preferred Gary Johnson to Clinton and Trump. You'd think he'd stop digging the hole he was in but his macho flashing didn't stop there, instead he doubled down and began to make remarks that made it seem as if he endorsed pedophilia after getting into an online argument about age of consent laws[29]. I don't think Vohra supports pedophilia, but he wasn't helping his cause any. If you think things such as pedophilia would end the lunacy, he then posted on one of his accounts that school shootings were bad and that school board shootings were good. Oh, and he also wrote a public letter praising the traitor Bradley Manning[30] who became a member of the domestic terrorist group Antifa after Obama granted him clemency.

The joke is ultimately on him though, he began to destroy the very organization he pledged to help strengthen. On April 1st (April Fool's Day), he issued a statement on Facebook that appeared at face value to be a an apology and letter of remorse, but instead was just another slap for Libertarians. Vohra concluded his letter saying "Taxation is theft, military 'service' is just enabling government's idiotic foreign policy, police are the only mechanism by which the drug war is carried out, government school teachers are enemy collaborators..." and the list goes on.

The unhealthy culture within the Libertarian Party meets almost cult like standards, where party loyalty meets extremes and to even question any part of the LP or its leadership is to announce you are a heretic. The LP social media team in April of 2017 tweeted out a quote from the Church of Satan, and as soon as the controversy erupted, numerous LP officials began to say that anyone that said anything negative of the Church of Satan was essentially not a true Libertarian[31]. There is a meme online of a dog wearing a hat, drinking some coffee while sitting in a house on fire. A few panels in and the dog is still smiling while the house burns around him. "This is fine," the dog says in the last panel. That is the best description of what being a Libertarian Party loyalist is like. The LP, at least in my opinion (and I could be wrong) will never elect a senator or a congressman, much less a President.

[28] http://libertyviral.com/vice-chair-lp-service-members-moralless-murderers/#axzz5DkaJCqHH

[29] http://independentpoliticalreport.com/2018/01/lnc-vice-chair-arvin-vohra-once-again-stirs-controversy-calls-for-removal-with-age-of-consent-comments/

[30] https://www.rt.com/usa/416214-chelsea-manning-senate-kremlin/

[31] http://www.freedomgulch.com/satanism-in-the-libertarian-party/

If they don't make you want to leave voluntarily, they already have enough crazy people who will harass you online and in person. In the mid 2000's, the Libertarian Party attempted to rebrand and reform their College Libertarian clubs on college campuses with a new organization called Young Libertarians of America. That organization was less about starting new chapters and getting college kids engaged, and more about going around online and deciding who was and wasn't a "real Libertarian" with one of their board members (a known online troll) whose job was entirely dedicated to vetting you. That was his entire biography listed on the website, he basically had spent the last thirty or so years of his life getting into spats with people because no one is libertarian enough to meet his muster, and if you weren't for crack cocaine vending machines in daycares, you weren't allowed in the club. I still feel bad that an organization that I, my brother, and so many friends of mine have been apart of has turned into such a shit-show. When a College Libertarians chapter at Liberty University opened up for the first time in campus history in 2016, members of the Virginia LP were excited to see new and young people get excited for the party. The state social media secretary however had a problem with it, saying publicly that Christians should give up their faith to serve the Libertarian party entirely or leave the LP. If that doesn't sound like crazy talk I don't know what is.

America deserves a marketplace of ideas and the expansion and viability of third parties is how that can be achieved. The LP asks too much and gives too little (which in their defense, the other parties do as well), and its role in the Liberty movement, despite higher name recognition thanks to the two Gary Johnson campaigns, is still unpopular among what seems the be the entire country. It's sad but true, I know many libertarians who are justified when they say stay away from the Libertarians. Maybe it can be fixed, maybe something will happen or someone will come along and make liberty win! Maybe is all I can say, what I do know is that there isn't one singular way to get the message of liberty out there because we tried that option, and the results are what we see today.

Chapter 13: Alt-Right vs Galt-Right

"The libertarian believes that the best and most wonderful social outcomes are not those planned, structured, and anticipated, but rather the opposite" ~Jeffrey Tucker

National Review contributor David French remembers coming home to find a picture of his then-seven year old's face in a gas chamber. The legion of Pepe the Frog trolls began to gather around the fringes of the Trump campaign online and took trolling to rather disturbing levels. French was already in their targets after it was rumored he was going to run for president as an independent conservative candidate after Trump sealed the Republican nomination after the Indiana primary. He didn't help himself either by also writing a SOS piece in hopes of convincing Mitt Romney, a man not entirely loved by conservatives still and an open and avid Trump basher either. The alt-right in it's infantile stages had French in their radars, waiting for him to do or say something to piss them off.

French finally began to see the hate manifest, in his words he recalls "calling out notorious Trump ally Ann Coulter [the one who wanted to drown libertarians] for aping the white-nationalist language and rhetoric of the so-called alt-right." Immediately his Twitter account was bombarded with these fringe lunatics mentioning his adopted African daughter, going as far as to call him a "race-cuck" and accuse him of "raising the enemy." His wife wasn't safe either, soon she started receiving pornographic images of her having sex with black men, even accusing her of sleeping with numerous black men while her husband was in the military serving in Iraq. This type of behavior was targeted at other conservatives such as Ben Shapiro and Erik Erickson just to name a few. The alt-right even bugged me for a while, with some individuals claiming I didn't support Trump because I would "get deported" which is funny because I'm an American citizen. I did a livestream with my friend Alex Merced in February of 2017 about the relevancy of the alt-right, receiving one comment which said, "What a fucking joke lolbertarians are. You guys are just making shit up to justify your own insecurities." The rest of the comments were just about how Alex and I were Mexicans pushing the "globalist agenda."

I think many conservatives and libertarians gave a pass to the alt-right because they were just a bunch of online douchebags. They could taunt you all they wanted, but we still paid more attention to the folks who tried to burn down Trump rallies in 2016 and then Antifa after the election who literally burned down schools and caused millions of dollars in damages as they rioted around the country. Some of these white nationalists behaved almost like sleeper agents within conservative circles however, and went unnoticed until Hillary Clinton finally gave recognition to the existence of the alt-right during a campaign speech, thus giving them a type of twisted legitimacy of sorts.

Conservative commentator Nick Fuentes was one of those who fell through the cracks. In a piece for *Vice News*[32], student activist and pundit Will Nardi of *Right Side*

---

[32] https://www.vice.com/en_us/article/d3wkvj/college-conservativism-and-the-alt-right

Broadcasting Network (*RSBN*) fame and *the Washington Examiner* detailed his interactions with Fuentes, who became one of the most outspoken alt-right figures in the country after the Charlottesville riot in 2017. When they first met, they were first mutually respectful towards each other as they found common ground attending a liberal university while rejecting liberal beliefs, Will states "Nick and I had that in common, we commiserated over our shared struggle. I didn't realize that Nick saw his struggle as a fight to preserve white identity. We just never talked about it."

The story continues as Will discussed his progression into conservative media in parallel to Fuentes' progression at *RSBN*. Will continues saying "Fuentes took a different approach [in terms of what was discussed on his show compared to Will's], bringing the underground politics and conspiracies of the alt-right into the mainstream...he argued anti-Muslim and anti-Semitic positions, and in April, called for people who worked at *CNN* to be hanged." This is the biggest identifier of the alt-right, they love to use violent rhetoric in everything they say. For the alt-right, they behave also in an near identical manner to progressives and their use of extreme identity politics. A leaked video of Fuentes showed him saying that, "If a white person slept with a black person, that makes them a degenerate." As a mixed race person, I know I was disgusted by this idiocy myself. You'd think that would have stopped him, but he doubled down and fell back to the protection of the alt-right across the web.

The alt-right isn't exclusive to white nationalists, I often just refer to them as ethno-nationalists. I do this because the beliefs of segregation, racial IQ's, and other progressive eugenic theories and beliefs are held by blacks, Asians, and even Tila Tequila. That is right, Tila from *MTV* is a nazi. I don't think anyone knows when it happened, but the self proclaimed "alt-reich queen" detailed in a *Daily News* article in 2016, went full alt-right all of a sudden, going as far as to write a manifesto titled *Why I Sympathize With Hitler*. She also took a swipe to personally piss me off by attempting to smear the legacy of one of my favorite actors of all time, Paul Walker, best known for the most epic *Fast and Furious* film series, claiming his fatal car crash was "ritualistic murder." The alt-right believes that people of different races aren't meant to live amongst each other because of genetic differences that make them prone to conflict. In my research of the alt-right I've met ethno-nationalists of different races and creeds, who have found brotherhood amongst each other in their shared hatred... of each other.

At CPAC in 2017, I shared a cheap dorm offered by a partnering conservative organization with some other students outside of D.C. for the week. There were a group of guys that just didn't hang out with the rest us, they had the "Richard Spencer" haircut, but no one wanted to assume anything of it just because now it was a meme online. One of the dudes, a Mexican guy, came over to my friends to talk. I don't remember where the conversation went, but out of nowhere this dude was calling himself nationalist and a neo-confederate and wanted to deport everyone that refused to speak english. Obviously, I grabbed my shit and left because that conversation was getting really freaking weird.

One of the other dudes said he was a libertarian, but according to him we could only achieve a libertarian society if we kicked out all the non-whites because "they don't respect liberty." By his standards, I guess I'm getting tossed out of his helicopter for failing the racial purity test.

For the longest time, many libertarians thought they were free from having to deal with the alt-right frenzy conservatives had to deal with. The joke was on us though, as soon as it seemed we were in the clear, the crazy people started popping up out of nowhere like it was coming out of style. Christopher Cantwell of the popular online show *Radical Agenda* was once a self-identified anarchist with a major crush on Chilean dictator Augusto Pinochet, who is best known for dropping communists and people he accused of being communists out of helicopters. Cantwell eventually just stopped kidding us all that he had libertarian beliefs and came out of the alt-right closet as a actual, loud and proud fascist. Cantwell became a national figure during the Charlottesville, Virginia riot in August, 2017. Elle Reeve from *Vice News*[33] covered Cantwell and the other alt-right protesters before and during the riot.

Asking when Cantwell got into the "race stuff", he answered citing the killings of Trayvon Martin and Mike Brown, saying that in "every case, it's some little black asshole behaving like a savage and he gets himself in trouble shockingly enough. Whatever problems I might have with my fellow white people, they generally are not inclined to such behavior and you have to take that into consideration when you need to decide how you want to organize your society." What was funny was that Cantwell was a very vocal Donald Trump supporter in 2016, but even considered Trump a sellout because he "gave his daughter to a jew."

"I don't think you can think about race the way I do and watch that Kushner [Jared Kushner, Donald Trump's son-in-law] bastard walk around with that beautiful girl," Cantwell said. I've never ended a friendship because of politics, but I have had to end multiple friendships because people I thought I knew ended up coming out in the open holding the same despicable beliefs as Cantwell. Mr. Chris "It's physical removal time!" Cantwell was always an asshole and his turn towards fascism wasn't a surprise to most people with half a brain. Websites that used to host good libertarian and conservative views, out of nowhere kicked out all the writers and replaced them with paleoconservatives (basically confederates), identitarians, and basically every other term for the alt-right. Christopher Chase Rachels, a libertarian writer and author of the book *Spontaneous Order: The Capitalist Case for a Stateless Society* shocked a ton of people when he released his next book almost a year later titled *White, Right, and Libertarian* [34]which had a cover featuring five hanging bodies from a helicopter (their faces had the emblems of communism, Antifa, feminism, and Islam) and shockingly, a credit saying the foreword was written by Hans-Hermann Hoppe.

[33] https://www.youtube.com/watch?v=RlrcB1sAN8I

[34] https://libertarianvindicator.com/2018/01/26/breaking-controversial-christopher-chase-rachels-book-cover-leaked/

Hoppe is another alt-right idol, whose theory of property rights gained popularity among the alt-right who took it to the extreme conclusion that it is completely cool to throw people out of helicopters. A bunch of alt-right kids went to the International Students For Liberty Conference in 2017 calling themselves the Hoppe Caucus and brought with them alt-right leader of the National Policy Institute, Richard Spencer, also known as the Nazi who got punched in the face at the Trump inauguration. Obviously things got out of hand and the SFL coordinators had to get security to remove Spencer from the hotel venue. There was a point to be made to that, the alt-right is as libertarian as communists are libertarian. When violence is somehow justified for everything you want, you have just broken the Golden Rule of libertarianism.

The alt-right (the white nationalists specifically) often cry about the death of Western Civilization, with many of them essentially preaching the gospel of the once wonderful land of Europe, where white people flourished and frolicked in the fields and everything was peaceful, until the Jews and the minorities came! Of course I am being sarcastic, but the alt-right obviously has no understanding of the driving forces of history because they have created a false utopian history and desire to achieve something that has never and will never exist because it is utopian in construct. Additionally, the alt-right is all about intentionally designed and organized societies; listen to them long enough and these goons are totally down with eugenics and socialism. Libertarians however believe in voluntary cooperation and spontaneous order of the market. At its heart, there is no desire for individual liberty at all within the alt-right. Jeffrey Tucker from The Foundation for Economic Education (FEE) put it best in an article titled *Five Differences Between the Alt-Right and Libertarianism*, saying bluntly "the alt-right knows who its enemies are, and the libertarians are among them." Before reading any further, go buy a copy of Jeffrey Tucker's book *Right Wing Collectivism: The Other Threat to Liberty* because it is the best historical and philosophical breakdown of populism and the alt-right you will probably ever read.

While the truth can give libertarians confidence in their effort to push away cancer of the alt-right, thanks to a loud, angry minority of morons, the damage has been done in the wake of Charlottesville. In an op-ed at the *Washington Post*, writer and editor at *Genius.com* Josh Ganz wrote an article titled *Libertarians Have More in Common With the Alt-Right Than They Want You to Think*[35], going on to reference Murray Rothbard's admiration for Republican and vocal anti-communist Senator Joseph McCarthy, and a ghost written series of racially charged newsletters targeting various ethnic groups in hopes of driving up disenfranchised southern whites into adapting anarchist beliefs in an effort to create a half baked, libertarian and populist fusion called "paleoconservatism."

[35] https://www.washingtonpost.com/news/posteverything/wp/2017/09/19/libertarians-have-more-in-common-with-the-alt-right-than-they-want-you-to-think/?utm_term=.d1793dbf984b

An article from the *Daily Beast* made the rounds titled *The Insidious Libertarian-to-Alt-Right Pipeline*[36] written by Matt Lewis, arguing that libertarians are one racist tirade away from becoming part of Cantwell's physical removal squad. Lewis juxtaposes his own arguments though with a quote from David Boaz of the Cato Institute, reminding us all that "people change ideologies all the time. Some libertarians become conservatives, some become welfarist liberals... Jason Kessler [the organizer of the Charlottesville rally] apparently was in Occupy Wall Street [and worked for Obama] before he became an alt-right leader. The original neocons were leftists first. Hillary was a Goldwater girl."

Lewis goes on to even allude that Barry Goldwater would have been considered to some degree alt-right if he were alive today (that really ticked me off like you wouldn't believe). Now, because of a few bad hombres, everyone who calls themselves a conservative or a libertarian is at some point accused of being a white supremacist or alt-right. I'm not even fully white and I've been called a white supremacist, and I despite every episode I've ever recorded, article I've ever written debating, debunking, deconstructing the alt-right, I have even been accused of being alt-right. This is the new "Nazi". It's just a slur word now people go around throwing at each other. Nick Gillespie, the editor at large for *Reason*, wrote an article debunking the claims of the "libertarian to alt-right pipeline" saying the alt-right "is an explicit rejection of the foundational libertarian beliefs..."

Jennifer Grossman from the Atlas Society coined a term I've grown fond of over the years. At Freedom Fest 2017 in Las Vegas, where I was speaking at a panel discussion on the topic of "Why Latinos Should Read Ayn Rand" Jennifer at one point said, "We need less alt-right and more Galt-right." She was channeling Ayn Rand's ultimate objectivist hero John Galt- the man, the myth, the force of nature from her book Atlas Shrugged who is the ultimate embodiment of the unbound and courageous spirit of rugged individualism.

Libertarianism is all about the individual and respect for that individual's natural rights and right to live freely. The alt-right, no matter what form or name it comes in, is no different than communism and every other totalitarian disease that has plagued mankind. It is a ideology that is doomed to fail because it goes against the driving force of history and facts of life. Man will always have a desire to be free.

[36] https://www.thedailybeast.com/the-insidious-libertarian-to-alt-right-pipeline

Chapter 14: Joan Holloway's Lessons for Libertarians

"The first step towards change is awareness. The second step is acceptance." ~*Nathaniel Branden*

People read too much into things; open up a Gab account and you're alt-right, say you love to listen to that dope mixtape from the musical *Hamilton* and somehow you support open borders. I had a friend literally send me an email after removing me from his Facebook list (I refuse to call it a "friends" list because it distorts the meaning of friends) to tell me how disappointed he was that I liked Donald Trump's Facebook page because now I supported fascism apparently. Everyone is so literal all the time, that is why I show people I get very close to a picture of Picasso's Guernica painting, to see how they react.

You can tell a lot about a person by how they react to seeing it for the first time if they haven't learned about it before. It is actually, in my humble opinion, a grotesque painting, and that is its intention because it is meant to be grotesque. The Guernica bombings in Spain during the Spanish civil war were absolutely disgusting, and that is what Picasso wanted to show. In an art appreciation class I took, the other students refused to be open to the meanings behind pictures, they saw it for what it literally was, never what it was meant to be. If a person tells me all they see are square like animals screaming, I know this person isn't someone I want to spend long periods of my time with, it'll simply go wasted if they can't at least utter the word "pain" when looking at that painting.

The AMC drama *Mad Men* is one of my favorite shows of all time. You watch *Criminal Minds*, a show with killers, rapists, and dead bodies and no one cares or calls you demented. You watch *Breaking Bad* and no one assumes you cook meth in a trailer. You say you watch *Mad Men* and you might as well tell the world you are a chronic smoker, alcoholic, and sexually deviant misogynist. Progressives love to hate *Mad Men* despite the fact the writers of the show were all women. I just don't get it, but progressives usually hate what they don't understand anyway.

The show follows the ad agency of Sterling, Cooper, Draper, Price in bustling New York City from the 1950's through early 70's. It had a cast full of characters, my favorite being Joan Holloway. Joan, the secretary turned eventual partner and eventual single mother/business owner near the end of the series, is thought of by casual watchers of the show as a rude and thoughtless sex object. For die hard *Mad Men* fans, you know that Joan is anything but a throwaway character. While most male viewers may have been infatuated with the actress Christina Hendrix's dangerous curves and Marilyn Monroe traits, you watch her story arc long enough and you realize Joan is the very definition of an Ayn Rand hero. I try and model my clothing style off of the dapper Don Draper (on a budget of course), think of what shrewd Roger Sterling would do in certain business situations, but often wonder how Joan would encounter the annoying obstacles of office politics which make up most of one's headache in the real world.

In panels and speeches regarding Ayn Rand and objectivism, I bring up the differences between the characters of Peter Keating and Howard Roark from *the Fountainhead*. Peter never knew what he wanted and always wanted what others wanted him to do. Howard on the other hand was disgusted by Peter's lack of individual drive, because Roark was a man who understood his own drive for happiness and didn't need it to be justified by others. In that specific conversation, Roark says to Peter "you've already made a mistake. By asking me. By asking anyone. Never ask people. Not about your work. Don't you know what you want? How can you stand it? Not to know." Joan is much like Roark, she never feels the need have to justify her desires and intentions to others. When new employees like the shy Peggy start off at the agency and ask Joan for advice on life, Joan will give it, but putting it bluntly is an understatement. She went far for a woman that only wanted the simple life of domesticity for a while, but she craved the fight and victory of working. Joan succeeded not only in a time where women weren't seen as equals or business leaders, but also as someone who wasn't popular or very liked by her peers for a time. Joan was respected by those that knew ego, action, and results were the fountainhead of progress.

Here are eight lessons from Joan Holloway[37] that every libertarian needs to take to heart if they want to not just help promote and implement better changes in government and society, but live a life more like Roark, and less like Peter Keating.

1. "These men, constantly building them up, and for what? Dinner and Jewelry? Who cares?"

Libertarians make certain individuals there own libertarian Jesus Christ, and for what? They will either disappear or disappoint eventually. Ego stroking your boss or leader doesn't do anyone any good. It is never wise to simply cozy up to someone in hopes of them being your friend or getting you in the spotlight. Many libertarians, despite their claims to be individualists, are really followers. Ironically, there is a character in *Mad Men* exactly like Peter Keating (perhaps more malicious), that being the young Peter Campbell. This Peter always wants to go to the lunch meetings, have a seat at the board meetings, and get close to those in power and remind them how great they are and how much he admires them. Where Peter benefits in praise, Joan benefits with patience and hard work. The fun of it all will come and go, but your work and results are a permanent testament to your character no honest person can deny.

One controversial episode involved Joan being requested by the partners at the agency to sleep with a obese and misogynistic client in order to score a contract, and in return they would make her a partner. At first Joan protests, but later shows up at the clients door ready and willing to do what needed to be done to get what she wanted. While this brings up many ethical issues regarding a person's worth and ethic, the

[37] the quotes were thoughtfully collected by Jillian Harding at thoughtcatolog.com

characters of *Mad Men* (the men in particular) use sex as a currency to gain favors and influence. While Don Draper can bed the neighborhood and no one will judge him, Joan is chastised by the men in her office who call her a whore after learning what she did to become a partner. Regardless as to the morality of the matter, the one issue that goes unaddressed by viewers is that when the men do what Joan did, no one cares, but for Joan to sleep with a client in order to seal the deal, it's an issue.

Did Joan care? Did she feel like she was less of a person? While she might have been treated as a sex object by her superiors and the client, she didn't allow her peers to bring her down knowing that they would have made the exact same choice if they were in the situation she was in. One sentence from the Fountainhead reminds me often of Joan's resilience in the face of judgement. The antagonist of the story, Toohey, says to Roark, "Why don't you tell me what you think of me? In any words you wish. No one will hear us," to which Roark replies, "But I don't think of you."

No person or institution, not socially constructed ethnic group or social class has power over you unless you grant it that power. Joan never thought of herself as anything less than a person worthy of respect because of her sheer work ethic and willingness to make hard choices, unlike the other girls on the show who are willingly tied down by standards set against them by their employers and society at large alike.

2. "Men don't take the time to end things. They ignore you until you insist on a declaration of hate."

In the world of politics you learn over time it isn't good to tell each individual you hate to go jump off a cliff or drop a toaster in their bathtub with them sitting in it. I've encountered people who I helped bring up from positions of obscurity into positions of prominence, and then once they no longer needed my help proceeded to shit talk me behind my back and then come begging for help when they can't get anywhere themselves. I've encountered people who were so competitive, even the accomplished ones who I admired grow jealous of others of less stature than them if they aren't getting attention constantly. The power and influence of politics is intoxicating, why else does the cartel do anything to stay afloat? In the realm of politics, never expect bad relationships to end cleanly, you may want to just cut someone out of your life but sadly you'll be forced to work with them again at some point. Never be the one to draw out an honest answer from a scumbag about why they are a scumbag. Sometimes you just have to leave it. You know the truth, they know the truth, just leave it and move on, they aren't worth the time or frustration.

This goes especially for people that spend hours fighting on Facebook or Twitter and then add on countless more hours fuming and staying angry about it. Word to the wise, no one has ever had their mind changed because of a longwinded Facebook debate. Because of the form in which online threads and chats appear, everyone is more likely to be hostile because we as humans take everything very literally at face value, and because of the nature of the internet where our friends and the world can view us with a microscope, we have to do whatever we can to "win" even when you get nothing when you "win." A wiseman once said you play stupid games you get stupid prizes

Never forget Godwin's law, which basically says that the longer and argument goes on while online, the odds of someone being called Hitler grows exponentially. We've all done it or been called Hitler at some point by some random Reddit user, its just so easy to whip out when you know nothing else will work, but oh well.

3. "I'm not the solution to your problems. I'm another problem"

As discussed in earlier chapters, never be that person that says libertarianism is the answer to everything. Libertarians have a love/hate relationship with hypothetical situations, but one thing is clear, no one in the realm of public policy has a monopoly on truth, and it is ok to say "I don't know" sometimes. Claiming you don't have the answer doesn't validate your opponent's argument, it simply claims that you don't have the answer now and at least you're being intellectually honest. There are aspects to libertarianism I don't like, and that doesn't make me or any other person any less of a libertarian because every worldview, system, and manifesto is to some degree full of schisms, contradictions, and flaws; libertarianism is too. Always be open to other ideas. I get smack talked by some libertarians because I'm open to supporting the ideas of Universal Basic Income[38] if it means eliminating most of our current welfare state, and Transhumanism (the philosophy of joining aspects of technology with man, pretty trippy stuff). I'm not even a devoted believer of the Non-Aggression Principle because theorists and others have distorted the definition of aggression over time, (*Six Reasons Libertarians Should Reject The Non-Aggression Principle*[39] by Matt Zwolinski is a great piece you should check out to decide for yourself, or send to your anarchist friends to trigger them), but even I don't deny all those ideas come with some serious baggage. Be honest, open, and patient with exploring concepts and ideas, never make them your god.

Joan, despite preaching the gospel of the 1950's housewife to her peers and subordinates, lived for years in an unhappy and abusive marriage. Even after her divorce she respected what marriage represents, but chose to live as a single mother and eventually run her own business. If Joan had continued to subject herself to something that made her miserable and still continue to tell others she was happy and everything was fine, the story would have gone a much more depressing way for her.

---

[38] http://redtea.com/money/five-facts-about-universal-basic-income/

[39] https://www.libertarianism.org/blog/six-reasons-libertarians-should-reject-non-aggression-principle

4. "This is why I don't allow crying in the break room. It erodes morale. There's a place to do that- like your apartment."

On the internet, socialists and libertarians have been shown to own much of the ongoing political conversation on social media. Most of which consists of two things, people sharing memes espousing their love of libertarianism, or people bitching about other libertarians. I don't care if you wanna boast or have fun or annoy everyone with your political jokes and crap, all that can be tolerated. Never complain, scream, or pitch a fit on social media. You represent more than yourself whether you believe it or not, and you poison the well with each rant and whining monologue. Go talk to someone that cares, because I don't care.

There are genuine reasons to be upset in life: your dog dies, grandpa croaks, you remember the cult classic Firefly is never coming back despite the great results the movie got and the cast want to come back and keep the series going. One thing I can say is that politics and campaigns are never worth crying over. There was one race I was attached to specifically a while back, where people were literally posting videos online of themselves crying and saying there whole lives were ruined because they lost an election. As a chronic political loser, being defeated isn't all that terrible. You lose nothing, life goes on exactly the same way it went on before you wanted to run for office, you need to simply accept defeat with dignity because if you let them see you bleed, that single memory will go down forever and you'll never outlive it.

5. "That's life, one minute you're on top of the world, the next minute some secretary is running you over with a lawn mower."

The libertarian utopia we all dream of will never be real because we have to accept the fact some people love the state and don't mind being slaves. That doesn't mean we can't make life better, but that doesn't mean that when things go well, bad things won't happen, and when they do it isn't the end of the world.

6. "They can't stand it. They'll drag you into the garbage out there. They just want you to be as miserable as they are. I say let them have it."

Collectivists on the left and right hate libertarians because by virtue of being a libertarian, you claim you own yourself. That open defiance can't exist in the utopian, statist paradise the collectivists want. They will do anything, literally anything to control, just look at the communist revolutions of the 20th century, they are literally willing to murder everyone in order to get their way. Be like Joan, "let them have it" and fight with the same vigor as they do, just don't ever forget why you are fighting.

116

7. "You want to be taken seriously? Stop dressing like a little girl."

For the love of God- shower, shave, and wear age appropriate clothing that is flattering. Stereotypes are around for a reason, you shouldn't feed into them even if they are inaccurate.

8. "One day you'll lose someone who's very important to you. You'll see. It's very painful."

Never forget the humanity of others, for each person at the end of the day thinks that what they are doing is the right thing as much as you do. Except Hillary Clinton, she isn't human or capable of feelings.

Chapter 15: Taco Trucks on Every Corner

"A creative man is motivated by his desire to achieve, not by the desire to beat others." ~Ayn Rand

"Robber barons who want to poison our food and put children back into factories as cheap labor," she told the class. It always amazed me to meet these social justice evangelicals at Liberty University, it just seemed like a place that due to its politics would deter some people from attending, but spend enough time on campus and you find the student population is more diverse in thought than the media portrays them.

I don't remember what class I was in with this girl, but she was just going on and on about raised minimum wage and socialized medicine and the entire time I was just wondering where in the Bible Jesus said to go to your neighbor at gunpoint to take his wages and to give it to someone else. I call it the "Gospel of Violent Jesus", because this is the Jesus Christ radicalized by both radical conservatives and progressives, in which everything Jesus said is used to justify state sponsored violence and coercion. This government tied gospel is used to advocate for socialized medicine, like what Republican John Kasich tried to pull when he labeled himself a "compassionate conservative" and said Medicaid expansion was biblical. The progressive left is hateful towards Christians but yells and screams and brings up the Bible selectively to advocate for open borders and socialized everything.

This is just one major cultural mechanism used against libertarians: the claim that we are ungodly, callous, cold hearted individuals. Libertarians don't preach voluntary exchange because we don't like being told what to do, we do so because voluntary cooperation allows free and innovative people to do what no centralized and stiff authority can. Besides, who said in a world where government doesn't force people to be charitable through taxation that people wouldn't try and take care of the less amongst them?

Gret Glyer is one of those examples the media and those that teach the Gospel of Violent Jesus will never talk about. Gret founded an online app called DonorSee, which allows people to donate to causes around the world and see video and photo results in real time. In 2013, Gret decided to leave the comfort of the first world United States and go become a humanitarian in Africa for the next three years, taking care of children, building homes, and even crowdfunding $100,000 himself to build a girls school in Malawi. Gret cites his Christian faith and belief in libertarian principles for starting DonorSee and leading to its success. Today, Donorsee has helped build sustainable homes for people in the third world, helped provide AIDS medication for those in need in developing countries, and even assist domestically when natural disasters occur. DonorSee is so effective at making charity cost effective and engaging for donors, that the Peace Corps has banned its employees from using the app.

John Mackey from Whole Foods, Peter Thiel from Paypal, Charles Koch, these are just some of the names of billionaires who come at life from a libertarian perspective who are titans in the business world while also being incredibly charitable individuals. Khan Academy, one of the most highly respected online education sites in the world, runs entirely off of private donations and provides lessons and assistance to millions of individuals around the globe for no cost at all. Libertarians understand that charity is only charity when it is given willingly from the giver to the recipient, unlike government social programs which simply take your money and essentially set it on fire when they decide to print more of it.

For crying out loud, the government made slavery and segregation law of the land; for most their history Democrats didn't even want to negotiate instituting anti-lynching laws because they were afraid it would make their base upset. Why does the state get a pass for everything but it's libertarians that are always made to be the villain? Most of what we are taught in schools about the industrial revolution is false too; you know what life was like before the industrial age? Life sucked, that's what life was like. Because of that era, we live longer, make more money, and live way more comfortably than any point in human history. As comedian Joe Rogan once said, "Poor people are fat. Think on that shit."

I don't think most Americans would think of the rapper Cardi B as the messenger for fiscal sanity we needed, but Washington better pay attention to a rant she posted on Twitter in mid 2018 right around tax season. After Ms. B did her taxes and realized she sent 40% of her income to the IRS, she went into full libertarian beast mode and went viral in minutes blowing minds and dropping some basic economics on the world, "I wanna know what you're doing with my fucking money," she said, oh so poetically. The world's attention was on her, "like when you donate to a kid from a foreign country, they give you updates what they doing with your donation. I want to know what you're doing with my fucking tax money, because I'm from New York and the streets is always dirty, we was just voted the dirtiest city in America." She continued to ask where her fucking money is but I think you get the point. Wait until she realizes that her tax money paid for a politician's mistress/intern to get a boob job and then the rest was spent to buy a million dollar missile to kill a one dollar terrorist in the Middle East.

What is hilarious sometimes is that libertarians are even accused of not just being evil and careless, but also of being too trusting and nice. When it comes to the position of open borders and unfettered immigration, libertarians are split down the middle. One school of thought says you can't have a country without a border, and the other says government has no right to deter freedom of movement. The argument aside, what libertarians do agree on when you separate the mechanics from the ethics is that free people should do what they see fit to improve upon their own lives voluntarily and peacefully in the marketplace.

I believe that the government has a duty to defend and maintain a border because nations are more than a series of interconnected economies, they are a body of laws and collective of cultures and the government has the right to protect its people. Do we need immigration reform? Sure, that is up for debate, but coming from a border town in Arizona, there are incredibly dangerous people that pose a threat to American citizens if let over. With that said, I'm talking about drug cartels and human traffickers, not taco trucks…

Allow me to tell you the story of the most embarrassing day of Latinos for Trump cofounder Marco Gutierrez's life. During the 2016 election, Gutierrez was stumping for Trump's wall on *MSNBC*. "My culture is a very dominant culture," said Gutierrez, "and it's imposing and it's causing problems, and if you don't do something about it you're going to have taco trucks on every corner." When I think of foreign threats to the homeland, the last thing I imagine is the threat of taco trucks on every corner, in fact that is a dream of mine to have the option of walking out of work and getting an authentic Mexican taco. In fact, who says it's just a Mexican taco and not a Korean BBQ taco or something else?

The beauty of America is that we are a gathering of free people who can make our way in the world from nothing into something, and it starts with the free will to do so and the voluntary cooperation of the marketplace to provide equality of opportunity, not equality of outcome. There was a beautiful article published in April of 2018 at the *Odyssey* titled *As A First Generation Bosnian-American, I Know Immigrants Are What Make America Great[40]*, written by first generation American Melina Dautovic, a student at the University of Georgia. Melina discusses how her family traveled from war torn Bosnia in the 90's escaping ethnic and religious violence so they could craft a better life for themselves in the United States. Towards the end of the article Melina says, "The negative association with the word immigrant is something that our society and world have to change. People who leave their countries don't do it just because they want to," which alone goes against the blanket stereotype created by some conservatives that all immigrants are welfare vampires sucking away at taxpayer money and bringing with them disease and cultural marxism. She continues, "They don't leave the comfort of familiarity of their home and move somewhere to abject poverty and want to stay in poverty." Immigrants are people, and like all people, some are bad and some are good, but we have to have some respect for their humanity. Regardless of your stance on immigration, hate the process, hate the laws, but don't hate the people. Racism, ethno-nationalism, and xenophobia are all forms of irrational collectivism which strips the individual of their identity, and ultimately their natural rights as living, breathing human beings.

If I walk outside and suddenly saw taco trucks on every corner, I'd consider that progress because now someone has a job and income to provide for themselves. Taco's

[40] https://www.theodysseyonline.com/immigrants-are-what-make-america-great

are also God's gift to mankind. We should strive to expand prosperity, and that starts with expanding individual liberty.

Chapter 16: Making Freedom Fun Again

"Libertarianism writ large was broader in its history and perhaps philosophical scope than the liberty movement. The liberty movement was broader in numbers and political influence than libertarianism had ever been in the United States or virtually anywhere else."
~Jack Hunter

There was a fad in the mid-2000's where these "health experts" convinced people they would lose weight and get cut if they only ate bananas. This banana diet fad was a stupid idea, but people still fell for it. There are other stupid fads I'm glad are dead, like when I was in middle school and kids literally walked around with pacifiers in their mouths. Where there are fads, there are stupid people willing to go along with them. Sadly, some fads can kill; and I'm talking about socialism.

Bernie Sanders was the biggest winner in 2016 in my opinion, he was abled to drag the Democratic Party farther left than anyone had ever been able to. The Democrats of the Scoop Jackson and Jack Kennedy days where they agreed tax cuts worked and communism was despicable has now been replaced by a Democratic Party that thinks Venezuela is a good economic model. Sadly, Sanders dragged many Republicans with him too in terms of his views on fair trade and tariffs. A certain Republican in the White House said at a campaign event that Bernie was wrong about many things, but "he was right on trade." Take a wild guess who that is.

No matter how many people starve, no matter how many civil liberties they lose, not matter how many families are destroyed and innocents are killed or put into slavery, the communist principles found in socialism and progressivism still have their virtuous and loud defenders in the public square ranging from academia as seen in SDS or in the editing halls of *CNN*. Numerous polls conducted in 2018 have even shown half of millennials are interested in implementing a socialist government within their lifetime.

Do these young people know what socialism is though? In school we were taught socialism was just a way of meeting the needs of everyone, and that the root of socialism was sharing everything so no one went without. There was no talk of how the socialist government of Cuba killed teachers who refused to teach books not approved by Castro. There are never any discussions in class to discuss the millions who died under the socialist experiments in China, Russia, and Cambodia. Students never see the mass burial pits where innocent men, women, and children are thrown in because they have outlived their purpose to the socialist cause. In May of 1948, late British Prime Minister Winston Churchill said "socialism is the philosophy of failure, the creed of ignorance, and the gospel of envy." Despite witnessing the radical collectivism seen under socialist Germany under the despicable Adolf Hitler, the British voted out Churchill after the war in order to pursue their own attempt at making socialism work. It wouldn't be until the 1980's that the "Iron Lady" herself, Conservative Prime Minister Margaret Thatcher, would take on the union cartels and socialists within her own government to not only fight the communists in the USSR's Iron Curtain over Europe but save the United Kingdom from falling into a state of total financial and social collapse.

Socialism, communism, statism, whatever "ism" it is seems to always be the easy fallback when it comes to granting government more and more power. It is unmistakable that freedom is hard to fight for, but even harder to maintain when the free populace doesn't value it at all. Ronald Reagan said it best, "freedom is only one generation away from extinction."

I was at a local Libertarian meet-up after work in 2016 during the summer at a cafe across town after a long day of work. Typically at this meet-up it was the same handful of attendees, but this time we had a new guy come over. This creepy old guy with two lazy eyes just showed up and was basically killing the vibe. He sat down at our long table in our reserved room and wouldn't talk to anyone. He just stared at the wall across from him as if he were frozen. At one point I turned to my brother Ryan and whispered "do you think he's breathing because he may have died and just gotten stuck that way. Anyway, I was talking about Hayek's social change theory (sexy topic, I know) and he walked over and started saying "why would people want freedom when they want to control you and can't be convinced?" Now in that moment he was reaching out to touch me in order to somehow drive the point you can't escape the creepy clutches of statism and conformity and I was totally freaked out and told him to step off, but when you think about it, that is a profound question.

Nihilism and apathy are the libertarian's greatest enemies. The wave of socialism seems like it is just getting higher and higher, gaining distance and closing in no matter how far lovers of liberty run from it. When you understand that most people view history in the cyclical manner in which communists do, where essentially capitalism will lead to a socialist revolution which will end in all-out communism, it seems that you have to completely rewire the way people see the world in order to even get them towards considering even for a second your way of thinking.

Libertarianism as a philosophy has been labeled by its opponents as careless, destructive, and inhumane, characteristics which couldn't be farther from the truth. By focusing on individual liberty, you respect and promote the individualism of all mankind. What it comes down to is selfishness as Ayn Rand characterized it; you selfishly protecting your freedom and property and respecting the right of others to be just as selfish. Freedom knows every race, sex, tongue, and escapes the grasp of every tyrant and leaps over every wall. History has shown the rise and fall of nations, and that no empire or civilization is guaranteed permanence. Murray Rothbard once said, "To be moral, an act must be free," and that is why libertarians respect free will as long as that freedom does not intrude on the liberties of others.

A friend once asked why we don't teach libertarianism in public schools, to which I replied "because if the kids knew, they would grow up and abolish public schools."

Utopianism however is a false god, and I'm not fooled into thinking we will ever arrive at "Libertopia." No my friends, the utopia I sometimes envision where guns come without permits, roads are privatized, and people can pursue their dreams of art and innovation without the fear of censorship or tyrannical regulators is too much to ask for. America, the land of the free, fought a war for independence over a small tax on tea, but now we tax ourselves in ways the King of England would have considered ridiculous.

However, I'm in no way convinced we are marching towards the drumbeat of totalitarianism either. The Washington Cartel and other totalitarians no longer have a monopoly on information no matter how hard they try, free people in today's modern age will always find what they are looking for. While the mainstream media paints the picture that the youth are socialists eating Tide Pods yet are smart enough to rightfully take away our Second Amendment and right to self defense, what I see on the ground tells a very different story. Students are taking back free speech and promoting academic freedom in ways we've never seen. The spirit of the original Tea Party movement now lives with a generation of journalists and activists who are organizing to make policy that promotes liberty. Liberty Republicans are still dictating much of the important discussions in the halls of power and dragging the vampires of the cartel into the light for the world to see. Entertainers, teachers, and everyday people are creating content that promotes the idea that freedom is always the best answer.

The revolutionary impact blockchain technology that was born out of Bitcoin has created a stake, driven through the heart of the draconian banking systems and central planners. This technology is reaching millions of unbanked people, and providing a source of income and trusted exchange to many in developing countries. We haven't even touched the surface with its potential, but I knew the moment I was able to tip a waiter in Bitcoin when I didn't have any cash on hand that this was going to change the world.

In April, 2009, God gave the world a gift in the form of the television show *Parks and Recreation* and the libertarian messiah Ron Swanson. That show alone has done more to bring more libertarians into the movement and show the world the inefficiencies of even local government probably more so than an every treaties, white paper, and lecture combined.

Most importantly, as other nations tilt towards to false swan song of globalism and fascism, there are still millions around the globe organizing together to promote solutions that can bring the poor out of poverty, the destitute out of despair, and the oppressed into prosperity. The gate holding back human potential has been kicked down and will never be able to remove this knowledge from the world.

You won't see them on the news or in the papers sadly, but libertarian activists are sacrificing themselves everyday for the cause of freedom. The Cuban Libertarian Party was targeted by the Castro regime, and as soon as they proved to be a viable political threat, many of their members were thrown in jail as political prisoners and others simply were coerced into abandoning the cause all together. Libertarians in Venezuela were also targeted by the government and thrown in jail, some of which were the family and friends of the Venezuelan students I met at Cato University. Even Bitcoin mining was outlawed when the government realized their citizens were using Bitcoin to bypass Venezuelan banks in order to make overseas purchases.

During an event in Arlington, Virginia in 2017, I moderated a panel on "How to Make Freedom Fun Again" with Jennifer Grossman from the Atlas Society, Logan

Albright of Free the People, and Congressman Garrett. The crowd wasn't just diverse in terms of young and old, black and white and everything in between, men and women, gay and straight, but it was diverse in ideas. For the record, there is that stereotype that women don't go to libertarian events; rest assured, there were plenty of women at this event, and they were all extremely beautiful, the men who attended can testify. By the end of the night we had even converted a Bernie bro into a full on libertarian. Yes, we talked politics and culture, but we had fun in the process and the audience had one Hell of a time too. People naturally want to go where the fun is. What is the point of being free if you're not happy and enjoying life?

I will concede one stereotype is true, some libertarians are the most pessimistic and serious people you'll ever meet. You've seen them online say things like "while you were watching football, Obama sent a drone to bomb a Pakistani wedding" or "how can we talk about a celebrity scandal when we have $21 trillion in debt?" I know this type because, sadly, I was this type of person. You focus so much on the constant abuse, injustice, and state sponsored crimes around the world and you almost feel as if you are the only person in the world that cares. It almost makes you forget to live life while you're busy trying to remind everyone to own and live their own. Libertarians say we don't want to tell people what to do, but we seem to tell people what to do pretty often.

So much of my early adult life was defined solely by politics, which I did enjoy but far too often I allowed it to lead me into unnecessary conflict and add on stress and commitments I didn't really have any business getting into to begin with. During an interview on the *Joey Clark Radio Hour* with Joey Clark, a Birmingham based radio host, he asked me "who is Remso outside of this all?" Honestly I was stumped, I couldn't divorce myself from my identity as a the political commentator. I love going to find new restaurants, I basically live in my local comic book store, I run a side business as a photographer; I do those things only because they bring joy to me.

Logan during one of his answers at the panel said "the best way to spread liberty is to tell a story." What better way than that? The lifestyle of freedom can only become a reality when you choose to embrace it.

Acknowledgments

I'd like to thank my parents for dealing with me. My favorite libertarian meme is of a mother and her son, wearing a baseball cap and regular shirt, walking along and the boy points ahead and says "look, mommy! Libertarians!" and the mother says "Don't look at them Ricky, I don't want you to be influenced by... Oh God No... Ricky!!!!" the panel scrolls down and now Ricky is wearing a Ron Paul t-shirt, Jeffrey Tucker's bow tie, and his face is now just ancap colors. The kid replies, "taxation is theft, no victim no crime, end the fed, it's too late mother, I have seen everything." It's absolutely hilarious, go look it up. Anyway, that meme is the perfect representation of what my parents have had to deal with.

Thank you to Julianna who believed I could finish this book when I didn't believe I could. I'd like to thank Kim Bouffard, Emily Meadows, and Matthew Reiad for taking the time to go through and help me edit this beast of a book hopefully someone will buy. Kelsey Kurtinitis edited the draft of my first book which will (thank God) never see the light of day because it sucked, for that she deserves credit. Thank you to my friend and publicist Gabriella Hoffman for her level headedness, patience, grit, and tenacity, along with always being there to listen when I need to rant for half an hour straight over the phone. Thank you to Jimmy Ellenburg, Becky Gerritson, Casey Cheap, and Sarah Hubal for standing by me when I didn't have a clue in the world what to do. Thank you to my friends and liberty warriors at Free the People who taught me the ins and outs of the ways of politics, Logan Albright (who also basically helped me graduate college), Josh Withrow who always gives great advice and tough truths, and Matt Kibbe who showed me through his work when I was young that advancing liberty can be fun.

Thank you to Kaytee Moyer who gave me the cash I needed to get a microphone when I was a broke college kid and everyone else thought my show, *the Remso Republic*, was going to be a flop. Thank you to Brian Suojanen for giving me a shot when I had no resume, Albert "Al" Billingsly for showing me what it is to fight the power, and Tom Garrett for showing me that old Goldwater saying "extremism in defense of liberty is no vice" is still alive and well. Special thanks to Jennifer Grossman who showed me faith and reason can exist together, and Larry Sharpe, Robert Sarvis, Nick Freitas, Shak Hill, Jenn Gray, Jason Stapleton, and Kevin McCormick for always putting up a fight.

None of this would be possible without the support of my brother Ryan, one of the most under-appreciated school choice and libertarian activists in the state of Virginia. Ryan was also the producer for the *Remso Republic* podcast and was instrumental in making it the success it was, along with all the other projects he helped on. There would be no *Remso Republic* without Ryan. Shoutout to my podcasting mentors Marc Clair from the *Lions of Liberty* and Johnny "Rocket" Adams of *the Johnny Rocket Launch Pad* for being there with me from the start.

Something I'd like to leave you with, if and only if you are a libertarian of any professional capacity or of any particular stripe. During my time working for different campaigns, I willingly took on many clients and candidates who didn't have a shot. I didn't do it for the money, because I knew the money probably wasn't going to show up, I did it because fighting is easy when the wind is at your back and the enemy is on the run. Everyone wants an easy fight because it means the odds of getting hit are already remarkably low. Many of the people I worked for weren't so lucky. They were shoe string campaigns, our opponents were heavily favored, we already had to work twice as hard and that was just to stay up to pace. It is easy to fight when you know you will win, it is difficult to fight when you don't know if you can do it or doubt your ability from the beginning. Campaigns are short term measures, snapshots in time, but messages live on past you. Sometimes when you lose you still win because your opponent didn't think you were going to take a serious swing anyway, sometimes the simple act of just putting up a fight is victory enough.

Remso W. Martinez

Remso is a journalist and libertarian commentator. Remso is a graduate of Marion Military Institute and earned his Bachelor's degree in US Government Politics and Policy from Liberty University. Through his efforts he has been a recipient of Being Libertarian's 2017 Jefferson Liberty Award, and his podcast the Remso Republic was a 2017 Podcast Awards nominee for best in news and politics. His articles have also been published at FreedomWorks, the Media Research Center, TheBlaze, and numerous other outlets.

Logan Albright

Logan Albright is a libertarian writer and economist. He currently serves as the Director of Research for Free the People Foundation, Head Writer for Fight the Power Productions, and Director of Fiscal Research for Capital Policy Analytics. In his spare time, he is a novelist, musician, and moustache enthusiast. He lives in Washington, DC.

Follow Remso online

Facebook
Https://facebook.com/remsoforva/

Instagram
Https://instagram.com/remso4va/

Twitter
Https://twitter.com/remsoforva/

Minds
Https://minds.com/remsorepublic/

Gab
Https://gab.ai/remsorepublic/

Steemit
Https://steemit.com/@remsorepublic

Made in the USA
Monee, IL
01 February 2020